Discipleship is the art and science of helping people find, follow, and fully become like Jesus. Discipleship happens as God's people show love, share truth and live life with one another, making new disciples along the way.

-Brandon Cox

NURTURING YOUR FAITH:
A GUIDE TO DISCIPLESHIP AND SPIRITUAL GROWTH

NICHOLAS A. ROBERTSON

NURTURING YOUR FAITH: A GUIDE TO DISCIPLESHIP AND SPIRITUAL GROWTH

Copyright © 2024 by Impact Online Institute.
Published by: Reason with Robdon

ISBN: 978-1-990266-56-0

Book Cover Design by: **Iconic Presence**

- All rights reserved soley by the author. No part of the book may be reproduced, stored in a retreival system or transmitted by any means (mechanical, electronic, photocopy, recording or otherwise) without the written permission of the author.
- All scriptures are taken from the Holy Bible, New Living Translation, copyright ©1996, 2004, 2007 by the Tyndale House Foundation. Used by permission of Tyndale House Publishers Inc., Carol Stream, IL 30188. All rights reserved.
- All definitions are taken from Vine's Expository Dictionary of Old and New Testament Words, copyright © 1997 by Thomas Neilson, Inc. Used by permission of Thomas Neilson Inc., Nashville, Tennessee. All rights reserved.

Book Author:

I am available to speak at your conferences, workshops, crusades, conventions, seminars, youth ministry, mentorship, men's ministry, couple's ministry and any other speaking engagement.

Author's Contact Details:

Email:	reasonwithrobdon@gmail.com
Follow us:	Reason with Robdon
FB, IG, YT, X	Reason with Robdon

TABLE OF CONTENTS

FOREWORD 11
PREFACE 13
IDENTITY IN CHRIST: 18
   Understanding What It Means to Be a Christian? 18
FINDING REDEMPTION: 25
   The Journey to Becoming a Christian 25
UNDERSTANDING SALVATION: 31
   The Gift of Redemption 31
WALKING IN LIGHT: 36
   Navigating the Pathway to Salvation 36
GOD'S REDEMPTION BLUEPRINT: 44
   Understanding the Plan of Salvation 44
A BRIDGE TO REDEMPTION: 49
   Embracing Salvation through Faith 49
THE URGENCY OF REDEMPTION: 54
   Understanding The Need to Be Saved 54
THE WAY OF REDEMPTION: 59
   What Are the Steps to Salvation? 59
THE GOOD NEWS UNVEILED: 63
   Understanding the Gospel 63
UNRAVELLING THE MYSTERY: 69
   Examining the Concept of Sin 69
THE ULTIMATE SACRIFICE: 73
   Exploring the Necessity of Jesus' Death 73
TRIUMPH OVER DEATH: 79

Understanding the Significance of Jesus' Resurrection -------- 79
RECOGNISING THE NEED: ------------------------------------ 83
    Understanding Why I Need a Saviour ------------------------- 83
THE DIVINE RESCUE: -- 88
    Exploring God's Redemptive Plan ------------------------------ 88
REDEEMING LOVE: -- 92
    Unveiling the Mission of the Saviour --------------------------- 92
THE COST OF GRACE: -- 96
    Exploring the Price of Redemption ----------------------------- 96
TURNING TOWARDS GRACE: ------------------------------- 100
    Understanding the Meaning of Repentance ------------------ 100
THE FREEDOM OF FORGIVENESS: ----------------------- 104
    Understanding the Essence of Forgiveness ------------------- 104
IMMERSED IN FAITH: --------------------------------------- 110
    Understanding Water Baptism and Its Significance --------- 110
SUBMERGED IN GRACE: ----------------------------------- 113
    Examining the Purpose of Baptism --------------------------- 113
HOLINESS IN ACTION: ------------------------------------- 116
    Exploring the Meaning of Sanctification ---------------------- 116
CHOSEN AS HEIRS: --- 119
    Exploring the Meaning of Adoption in Christ --------------- 119
FROM DARKNESS TO LIGHT: ----------------------------- 123
    Unveiling the Power of Regeneration ------------------------- 123
CLOTHED IN ETERNAL SPLENDOUR: ------------------- 127
    Exploring the Meaning of Glorification ---------------------- 127
FOLLOWING IN HIS FOOTSTEPS: ------------------------ 133
    Understanding the Identity of a Disciple --------------------- 133

LIVING IN RIGHTEOUSNESS:	137
Understanding the Concept of Moral Excellence	137
THE CALL TO PURITY:	140
Understanding the Concept of Holiness	140
INFINITE MAJESTY:	144
Discovering the Identity of God	144
DECLARED RIGHTEOUS:	151
Exploring the idea of justification	151
THE SON OF GOD:	155
Understanding the Identity of Jesus Christ	155
THE DIVINE COMFORTER:	159
Exploring the Identity of the Holy Spirit	159
THE MYSTERY OF THREE IN ONE:	166
Exploring the Concept of the Trinity	166
THE COMMUNITY OF BELIEVERS:	169
Investigating the Identity of the Church	169
LIVING IN VICTORY:	171
Embracing Your Identity in Christ	171
THE HEART OF SERVICE:	174
Exploring the Meaning of Servanthood	174
WALKING IN TRANSPARENCY:	177
Understanding the Importance of Accountability	177
THE POWER OF YIELDING:	179
Understanding the Joy of Submission	179
CULTIVATING DISCIPLINE:	182
Navigating the Path to Spiritual Growth	182
BEARING WITNESS:	186

- Understanding the Power of a Christian Testimony -------- 186
- CRAFTING YOUR STORY: ------------------------------------ 190
  - A Guide to Sharing Your Testimony ------------------------ 190
- BEARING WITNESS: -- 195
  - Sharing Your Testimony with Boldness and Grace ---------- 195
- COMMUNING WITH GOD: --------------------------------------- 201
  - Unveiling the Purpose of Prayer -------------------------- 201
- THE POWER OF PETITION: ------------------------------------ 204
  - Examining the Purpose of Prayer -------------------------- 204
- THE ART OF EFFECTIVE PRAYER: ------------------------------ 206
  - Mastering the Language of the Heart ---------------------- 206
- THE SUBSTANCE OF HOPE: ------------------------------------ 209
  - Unravelling the Meaning of Faith ------------------------- 209
- SURRENDERING TO SOVEREIGNTY: ------------------------------ 213
  - Learning to Trust God Completely ------------------------- 213
- THE SACRED SCRIPTURES: ------------------------------------ 217
  - Examining the Bible -------------------------------------- 217
- THE VERACITY OF SCRIPTURE: -------------------------------- 221
  - Exploring the Foundation of Belief in the Bible --------- 221
- ILLUMINATING TRUTH: --------------------------------------- 225
  - Exploring the Purpose of the Bible ----------------------- 225
- HEARTFELT DEVOTION: --------------------------------------- 228
  - Understanding the Meaning of Worship --------------------- 228
- THE HEART OF WORSHIP: ------------------------------------- 231
  - Exploring the Heart of True Devotion --------------------- 231
- EXALTING THE ALMIGHTY: ------------------------------------ 234
  - Understanding the Meaning of Praise ---------------------- 234

GRATITUDE IN ACTION: -------------------------------------- 240
    Exploring the Meaning of Thankfulness ---------------------- 240
UNDERSTANDING SEXUAL PURITY: -------------------- 243
    Exploring the Concept of Sexual Immorality----------------- 243
GUARDING THE HEART: ------------------------------------ 247
    Understanding the Importance of Sexual Purity ------------- 247
THE TEMPTATION OF LUST: ------------------------------ 251
    Understanding Its Nature and Consequences ---------------- 251
EXPLORING ROMANTIC CONNECTIONS: --------------- 254
    Exploring the Dynamics of Dating---------------------------- 254
THE SACRED UNION: --- 259
    Exploring the Essence of Marriage--------------------------- 259
THE DECEPTIVE SNARE: ------------------------------------- 262
    Understanding the Nature of Pride --------------------------- 262
THE FIERY EMOTION: -- 265
    Understanding the Nature of Anger -------------------------- 265
THE DIGNITY OF LABOUR: --------------------------------- 269
    Exploring the Role of Work for Christians -------------------- 269
RESPONSIBLE GUARDIANSHIP: --------------------------- 272
    Understanding the Concept of Stewardship ----------------- 272
THE JOY OF GENEROSITY: ---------------------------------- 276
    Exploring the Meaning of Giving ----------------------------- 276
HONOURING GOD WITH OUR FINANCES: ------------- 279
    Exploring Biblical Principles of Tithing ------------------------ 279
UNMASKING THE ENEMY: ----------------------------------- 282
    Exploring the Identity of Satan ------------------------------- 282
CULTIVATING EXCELLENCE: --------------------------------- 287

    Nurturing Strong Work Ethic --- 287
THE SACRED FEAST: --- 291
    Exploring the Meaning of Holy Communion --- 291
THE STRENGTH OF MEEKNESS: --- 294
    Understanding the Virtue of Humility --- 294
BALANCE AND MODERATION: --- 298
    Exploring the Concept of Temperance --- 298
ENDURANCE IN ADVERSITY: --- 301
    Understanding the Notion of Longsuffering --- 301
THE LANGUAGE OF THE HEART: --- 304
    Examining the Meaning of Love --- 304
JOURNEYING IN TRUST: --- 307
    Understanding the Meaning of Walking by Faith --- 307
THE LANGUAGE OF THE SPIRIT: --- 310
    Exploring the Gift of Speaking in Tongues --- 310
HEALING BROKEN BONDS: --- 313
    Exploring the Meaning of Reconciliation --- 313
CLEANSING THE SOUL: --- 316
    Understanding the Purpose of Confession --- 316
METAMORPHOSIS OF THE SOUL: --- 319
    Exploring the Transformative Power of Conversion --- 319
SHARING THE LIGHT: --- 322
    Understanding the Art of Effective Witnessing --- 322
LIBERATED BY GRACE: --- 325
    Understanding Divine Deliverance --- 325
ENGAGING IN SPIRITUAL BATTLE: --- 328
    Examining the Practice of Casting Out Demons --- 328

FOREWORD

Welcome to "Nurturing Your Faith: A Guide to Discipleship and Spiritual Growth." As you hold this guide in your hands, you are embarking on a journey—an adventure into the depths of your soul and the heart of your faith. In these pages, you will find a roadmap for nurturing and cultivating your relationship with God, for deepening your understanding of Scripture, and for growing as a disciple of Christ.

Discipleship is not merely a passive journey; it is an active pursuit of God's heart—a daily commitment to seeking Him, knowing Him, and following Him wholeheartedly. This guide is designed to accompany you on this journey, offering insights, reflections, and practical tools to aid you in your spiritual growth.

As you engage with the material presented here, I encourage you to approach it with an open heart and a teachable spirit. Allow yourself to be challenged, to be stretched, and to be transformed by the truths you encounter. And remember, you are not alone on this journey. God is with you every step of the way, guiding you, sustaining you, and empowering you to become the person He created you to be.

May this guide serve as a beacon of light on your path, illuminating the way forward and inspiring you to press on toward the goal of knowing Christ more deeply. May it ignite a passion for discipleship within you and spur you on to greater spiritual growth and maturity.

May your faith journey be richly blessed, and may you experience the abundant life that comes from walking closely with the Saviour.

In His service,
Danielle Brown- Robertson,
Author, Counsellor, Minister.

PREFACE

In the intricate embroidery of faith, there lies an essential thread that binds believers together: the journey of discipleship. The pursuit of spiritual growth, understanding, and an unwavering commitment to living out the tenets of faith form the foundation of this expedition. It is the process of following Jesus Christ, learning from Him, and growing in relationship with Him. It involves not only believing in Jesus as Saviour but also committing to becoming more like Him in character, attitude, and actions. Discipleship encompasses both a personal journey of spiritual growth and a communal aspect of living out one's faith in community with other believers.

Critical aspects of discipleship include:

- **Following Jesus:** At its core, discipleship involves following the example and teachings of Jesus Christ. This means priority. Sing His will and His ways above our own desires and preferences.

- **Learning from Jesus:** Discipleship entails studying and meditating on the Word of God (the Bible) to understand Jesus' teachings, principles, and values. It also involves seeking guidance from the Holy Spirit and allowing Him to transform our minds and hearts.

- **Imitating Christ:** As disciples, we are called to imitate the character of Jesus Christ. This includes demonstrating love, compassion, humility, forgiveness, and obedience in our interactions with others.

- **Growth and Transformation:** Discipleship is a lifelong journey of growth and transformation. It involves continually surrendering to God's will, allowing Him to mould us into the image of Christ, and overcoming areas of weakness and sin through the power of the Holy Spirit.

- **Making Disciples:** Part of discipleship is sharing the good news of Jesus Christ with others and helping them grow in their own faith journey. This involves mentoring, teaching, encouraging, and supporting others as they seek to become disciples of Jesus.

Ultimately, discipleship is about becoming more like Jesus Christ in every aspect of our lives—loving God with all our heart, soul, mind, and strength, and loving our neighbours as ourselves. It's a transformative process that shapes our identity, our relationships, and our purpose in life.

"The Disciple" typically refers to a follower or student of a religious leader or teacher, particularly in the context of Christianity. In the New Testament, Jesus had many disciples who followed Him, learned from His teachings, and sought to emulate His example. The term "disciple" comes from the Greek word "mathētēs," which means learner or pupil.

In Christianity, discipleship involves not only believing in Jesus as Saviour but also committing to follow Him wholeheartedly, learning from His teachings, and growing in relationship with Him. Discipleship is a transformative journey of spiritual growth, characterised by obedience to Jesus' commands, love for God and others, and a desire to make more disciples.

Throughout the New Testament, various individuals are depicted as disciples of Jesus, including the twelve apostles (such as Peter, James, John, and Matthew) and other followers who devoted themselves to Jesus' teachings and mission. These disciples were witnesses to Jesus' ministry, miracles, death, and resurrection, and they played crucial roles in spreading the message of the Gospel after His ascension.

In broader terms, "disciple" can also refer to any believer in Jesus Christ who seeks to follow Him faithfully, learn from

His teachings, and grow in spiritual maturity. Discipleship is not merely about acquiring knowledge but also about living out the principles and values of the Kingdom of God in everyday life, empowered by the Holy Spirit.

Discipleship is critical to our Christian purpose and therefore must be thoroughly examined to empower the student and equip the teacher.

As we go aboard on this literary endeavour, my heart resonates with the profound importance of effective discipleship. This book is not just a collection of principles; rather, it is a roadmap crafted to guide believers in their quest for a deeper correlation with their faith. It is a labour of love born from a passion for nurturing spiritual growth and empowering individuals to walk steadfastly on the path of discipleship.

"Nurturing Your Faith: A Guide to Discipleship and Spiritual Growth" is an exploration into the foundational elements that fuel the growth and maturity of every believer. Within these pages, you'll find a mosaic of insights, practical wisdom, and actionable steps distilled from the collective wisdom of spiritual mentors, scholars, and personal experiences.

The intent of this book is simple yet profound: to equip believers with the necessary tools to flourish in their faith journey. Whether you're at the threshold of your spiritual expedition or have traversed considerable distances, my hope is that these words will resonate with your soul, ignite your spirit, and invigorate your pursuit of spiritual excellence.

I am profoundly grateful for the opportunity to share this odyssey of faith with you. As we delve into the critical keys together, may this book serve as a guiding light, illuminating the path toward a more profound understanding, a richer faith, and a life deeply rooted in discipleship.

Yours Truly,
Nicholas Robertson,
Your Faith Partner.

IDENTITY IN CHRIST:
Understanding What It Means to Be a Christian?

"God will meet you where you are in order to take you where He wants you to go."- Tony Evans

The dictionary defines a Christian typically as someone who professes belief in Jesus Christ or follows the teachings derived from Him. Yet, this definition often fails to capture the deeper essence of what it truly means to be a Christian according to biblical teachings. The term "Christian" itself appears three times in the New Testament (Acts 11:26; 26:28; 1 Peter 4:16). Initially used in Antioch, it signified followers of Christ whose conduct, actions, and speech mirrored that of Jesus. Literally, the term "Christian" denotes belonging to the party or following of Christ. Over time, however, its significance has dwindled, leading to misconceptions wherein people associate being a Christian with mere religiosity or moral values, irrespective of genuine allegiance to Christ.

Merely attending church, performing charitable deeds, or possessing ethical virtues doesn't inherently define someone as a Christian. The Bible underscores that salvation isn't earned through good works but is a result of God's mercy and the transformative work of the Holy Spirit (Titus 3:5). A genuine Christian, therefore, is someone reborn through God's grace, placing unwavering trust in Jesus Christ (John 3:3; John 3:7; 1 Peter 1:23). Ephesians 2:8 reinforces this notion, emphasising salvation as a gift received through faith and grace.

Crucially, a true Christian manifests faith and trust in the person and sacrificial work of Jesus Christ, including His crucifixion for sins and resurrection. Such faith grants the privilege of becoming children of God (John 1:12). The hallmark of a genuine Christian lies in their love for others and their obedience to God's Word (1 John 2:4, 10), signifying their status as part of God's family and recipients of new life in Christ.

Interestingly, the label "Christian" was initially coined by Gentiles in Antioch and might have been intended as a mockery (Acts 11:26). In the New Testament, believers often referred to themselves as brethren, disciples, or saints rather than Christians. This nomenclature arose during a period of rapid expansion in the church when believers dispersed due to persecution, spreading the gospel to various regions.

Ancient Greeks were accustomed to assigning satirical nicknames to groups, like "Pompeians" or "Sullanians." Similarly, the term "Christian" was a playful, dismissive gesture, bestowed upon those centred around Christ in their conduct and speech.

The word "Christ" held little significance for the general populace immediately after Jesus' resurrection, resulting in varied interpretations of believers as "Chrestians" associated with a figure called "Chrestus." This ambiguity hints at the likelihood of outsiders creating the term "Christian" without an in-depth understanding of the faith.

Jewish non-believers wouldn't have used "Christian" due to their rejection of Jesus as the Messiah. In the book of Acts, these individuals referred to Christians as those of the Nazarene sect. Consequently, the term "Christian" likely originated as a derisive insult.

Even the Bible suggests that "Christian" might have initially been a mocking insult, as seen in Peter's instruction not to be ashamed if labelled as such (1 Peter 4:16). Herod Agrippa's retort to Paul further emphasises the negative connotation associated with the term (Acts 26:28).

In summary, the term "Christian" initially emerged as a label attributed to those imitating Christ but might have evolved as a disparaging epithet crafted by outsiders. Its derogatory origins notwithstanding, it has come to symbolise genuine devotion to Christ among believers worldwide.

Dear reader,
Being a Christian transcends mere identity; it's a profound commitment to faithfully serve God and live out His teachings. Central to this commitment is the imperative to share the Gospel with others, serving as a beacon of light and inspiration. By sharing the transformative message of Christ's love and salvation, we not only fulfil our duty as believers but also have the opportunity to inspire others to join us in the journey of faith. Let us embrace our calling with fervour, spreading the message of hope and redemption to all who cross our paths.

Activity: Exploring What It Means to Be a Christian

Objective: The objective of this activity is to facilitate personal reflection and exploration of key aspects of Christian faith and practice.

Instructions:

- Take some time to reflect on each question or prompt provided below.
- Write down your thoughts and any questions that come to mind.
- Be open and honest with yourself as you engage in this reflection process.
- After completing the activity, consider discussing your responses with a trusted friend, mentor, or spiritual advisor for further insight and guidance.

Task:

1. What does being a Christian mean to you personally?

_____

_____

_____

2. Reflect on your understanding of God. How do you perceive God's character, attributes, and relationship with humanity?

_____

_____

_____

3. Consider the significance of Jesus Christ in your faith. What does Jesus' life, teachings, death, and resurrection mean to you?

4. Explore the role of the Holy Spirit in your life. How do you experience the presence and guidance of the Holy Spirit?

5. Think about your practices of prayer and worship. How do these spiritual disciplines nurture your relationship with God?

6. Reflect on the ethical teachings of Christianity. How do you strive to live out the values of love, compassion, forgiveness, and justice in your daily life?

7. Consider the community aspect of Christianity. How do you engage with fellow believers and contribute to the life of your faith community?

8. Reflect on your journey of faith. What challenges have you faced, and how have you grown spiritually through those experiences?

_____
_____
_____

9. What questions or uncertainties do you have about your faith? Are there areas where you desire deeper understanding or clarity?

_____
_____
_____

10. How do you envision your ongoing journey as a Christian? What aspirations or goals do you have for your spiritual growth and development?

Reflection:
Take a moment to consider how you can apply what you've learned to deepen your relationship with God and live out your faith more fully in your daily life.

FINDING REDEMPTION:
The Journey to Becoming a Christian

"God never said that the journey would be easy, but He did say that the arrival would be worthwhile."

Becoming a Christian

Becoming a Christian is a personal journey of faith and transformation. It begins with acknowledging your need for salvation and recognising Jesus Christ as the Son of God who died for your sins and rose again. You can become a Christian by repenting of your sins, confessing your faith in Jesus Christ as your Lord and Saviour, and inviting Him into your life. This can be done through prayer expressing your desire to follow Jesus and asking for forgiveness of your sins. As you surrender your life to Christ, you should commit to reading and studying the Bible, pray regularly, and seek fellowship with other believers in a local Christian community. As you embrace your new identity as a child of God, allow the Holy Spirit to guide you on your journey of faith, growth, and discipleship. Becoming a Christian is not just about a one-time decision, but a lifelong commitment to follow Jesus and live according to His teachings. The journey to Christianity requires you to understand the essence of what it means to be called a "Christian."

Who is a Christian?

This term "Christian" trace back to Antioch in the first century A.D. (Acts 11:26). Initially, it was intended to be an insult, meaning "little Christ." However, believers embraced it over time, using it to denote their allegiance to Jesus Christ. In its simplest form, a Christian is someone who follows Jesus Christ.

Why Should You Become a Christian?

Jesus paid our ransom to liberate us from bondage. He proclaimed, "I did not come to be served, but to serve, and to give His life as a ransom for many" (Mark 10:45). This concept of a ransom involves a payment made for someone's release, often seen in cases of kidnapping where a sum is paid for the freedom of a captive. We found ourselves bound by our sins, but what does this bondage entail? It's the captivity to sin and its dire consequences—death followed by eternal separation from God. Therefore, we required a ransom, and Christ became that ransom.

Why was this ransom necessary?

This was relevant because all of us are tainted by sin (Romans 3:23), making us liable to God's judgment (Romans 6:23). Jesus settled this ransom by sacrificing Himself on the cross for our sins (1 Corinthians 15:3; 2 Corinthians 5:21). His death holds the power to atone for our transgressions. How was His death significant enough to cover all our sins? Jesus, being God in human form, came to earth to identify with us and offer Himself for our sins (John 1:1,14). His divinity rendered His death infinitely valuable, enough to absolve the world's sins (1 John 2:2). His resurrection proved the sufficiency of His sacrifice and His triumph over sin and death.

How to become a Christianity?

This is the beauty of it. In His love for us, God made the path to Christianity remarkably simple. All it takes is accepting Jesus as your Saviour, fully acknowledging His death as the perfect payment for your sins (John 3:16), placing complete trust in Him as your Saviour alone (John 14:6; Acts 4:12). Becoming a Christian isn't about rituals, church attendance, or specific actions and abstentions. It's about nurturing a personal relationship with Jesus Christ. Faith in Christ forms the core of being a Christian.

Are You Ready to Embrace Christianity?

Christianity involves a personal journey of faith and commitment to following Jesus Christ. If you're prepared to embrace Christianity by receiving Jesus Christ as your Saviour, it's a matter of belief:

- Do you comprehend and believe that you've sinned and face God's judgment?
- Do you recognise and believe that Jesus took your punishment upon Himself, dying in your place?

- Do you grasp and believe that His death sufficed to pay for your sins?

If your responses to these questions are affirmative, then place your trust wholly in Jesus as your Saviour. Embrace Him through faith, entrusting in Him alone. Embracing Christianity is ultimately about surrendering your life to Jesus Christ, receiving His grace and forgiveness, and living in obedience to Him. It's a journey of faith, guided by the Holy Spirit, that leads to abundant life now and eternal life with God in the future.

Dear reader,

The journey to becoming a Christian is a personal quest marked by faith and inner transformation. It involves encountering the message of Christ's love and sacrifice, prompting individuals to reassess their beliefs and values. Through prayer, reflection, and guidance from Scripture, individuals set out on a journey of spiritual growth and renewal, experiencing moments of surrender and conviction. Embracing Christianity means undergoing an inward change that aligns one's life with God's will and purpose. If you haven't embraced Christianity yet, you can accept Him today. And if you're already a Christian, endeavour to invite others to embrace faith in God. As you engage with this resource, you'll be empowered to share your faith with others.

The Journey to Becoming a Christian - Reflective Activity

Objective: This activity aims to encourage personal reflection on the journey of becoming a Christian and the key elements involved in this process.

Instructions:
- Reflect on each question provided below.
- Write down your thoughts, feelings, and any insights that come to mind.
- Take your time and be honest with yourself as you engage in this reflective process.
- After completing the activity, consider discussing your responses with a friend, mentor, or spiritual advisor for further insight and support.

Activity Questions:

1. What initially drew you to explore Christianity or consider becoming a Christian?

   _____

   _____

   _____

2. Reflect on the moment or experience when you made the decision to become a Christian. What factors influenced your decision, and how did you feel at that time?

   _____

   _____

   _____

3. Consider the key elements of your journey to becoming a Christian, such as learning about Jesus Christ,

understanding Christian beliefs, participating in worship or fellowship, or experiencing a personal encounter with God. Which of these elements have been most significant for you, and why?

_____

_____

_____

4. Reflect on your life since becoming a Christian. How has your faith journey unfolded, and what transformations or growth have you experienced along the way?

_____

_____

_____

Reflection:

Take a moment to review how your journey to becoming a Christian has shaped your identity, beliefs, and relationship with God. Consider how you can continue to nurture and deepen your faith as you journey forward.

UNDERSTANDING SALVATION:
The Gift of Redemption

"There is nothing more important than your eternal salvation." — Kirk Cameron

Salvation signifies being rescued from peril or suffering. To save means to protect or deliver, encompassing the notions of triumph, well-being, and preservation. Salvation, from a Christian perspective refers to the deliverance of individuals from sin and its consequences, eventually leading to eternal life with God.

While the term "saved" or "salvation" in the Bible can refer to immediate physical deliverance like Paul's release from prison (Philippians 1:19), its primary focus is on everlasting spiritual liberation.

In Acts 16:30-31, the jailer, after witnessing an earthquake that miraculously freed Paul and Silas from their chains, asks them, "Sirs, what must I do to be saved?"

Paul and Silas respond: "Believe in the Lord Jesus, and you will be saved—you and your household."

In response to the jailer passionate query, Paul instructed the Philippian jailer on how to attain salvation. This involves acknowledging Jesus as the Son of God, accepting his teachings, and recognising His sacrificial death and resurrection as the means of reconciliation between humanity and God. Salvation is therefore about establishing fellowship with God.

To gain a deeper understanding of salvation, I'll share a story that was told to me years ago. Once upon a time, there was a traveller named Jack who lived in a beautiful but dangerous land. This land was filled with treacherous paths, deep valleys, and dark forests. Despite the dangers, Jack loved to explore and journey through the land, always seeking new adventures.

One day, while wandering through a dense forest, Jack became lost. He stumbled upon a steep cliff and found himself dangling on the edge, clinging to a small tree branch. Below him was a bottomless chasm, and he knew that without help, he would surely fall to his doom.

Jack cried out for help, but no one seemed to hear him. He realised that he was trapped and helpless to save himself. Just when he thought all hope was lost, a guide appeared. The guide reached out a strong hand and pulled Jack to safety.

Grateful for his rescue, Jack asked the guide how he could repay him. The guide explained that he didn't need repayment but offered Jack a map and a compass to help him navigate the dangerous land safely. He also promised to accompany Jack on his journey, guiding him through every perilous path.

Jack realised that he couldn't survive in this land on his own. He needed the guide's help to navigate the dangers and reach safety. With the guide by his side, Jack embarked on a new journey, knowing that he was no longer alone and that he had found the salvation he desperately needed.

In this story, Jack represents humanity, and the dangerous land symbolises the world filled with sin and its consequences. Just like Jack needed a guide to rescue him from the dangers of the land, we all need salvation to rescue us from the consequences of sin. Without salvation, we are lost and helpless, but with it, we find hope, guidance, and a new life. Salvation rescues us from the "wrath of God," that is, His judgment of sin (Romans 5:9; 1 Thessalonians 5:9). Our wrongdoing (transgression of God's expectations) has distanced us from God, and its consequence is death (Romans 6:23). Salvation, God's gift to us involves freeing us from sin's outcome and entails the elimination of sin's dominion and punishment.

Only God can eradicate sin and absolve us from its penalty (2 Timothy 1:9; Titus 3:5). God has delivered us through Jesus Christ (John 3:17). Specifically, Jesus' crucifixion and subsequent resurrection secured our salvation (Romans 5:10; Ephesians 1:7). Salvation is God's gracious, unmerited gift (Ephesians 2:5, 8) and is solely attainable through faith in Jesus Christ (Acts 4:12). Salvation comes through faith. Initially, we hear the gospel—the news of Jesus' death and resurrection (Ephesians 1:13). Then, we must believe. That is, we wholeheartedly trust in the Lord Jesus (Romans 1:16). Sincerely believing God involves repentance, a change of perspective regarding sin and Christ (Acts 3:19).

A concise description of salvation would be "God's grace-given liberation from eternal punishment for sin, bestowed upon those who embrace, through faith, God's terms of repentance and belief in the Lord Jesus." Salvation is exclusively found in Jesus (John 14:6; Acts 4:12) and relies entirely on God for provision and certainty.

Dear reader,
The most significant blessing we possess is eternal salvation. Choose to live a life of holiness today and for all eternity.

The Gift of Redemption - Reflective Activity

Objective: This activity aims to facilitate personal reflection on the profound gift of redemption offered through Jesus Christ.

Instructions:
- Reflect on each question provided below.
- In the space provided, write down your thoughts, feelings, and any insights that come to mind.
- Take your time and be honest with yourself as you engage in this reflective process.
- After completing the activity, consider discussing your responses with a friend, mentor, or spiritual advisor for further insight and support.

Activity Question:

1. What does redemption mean to you personally, and how has it impacted your life?

_____

_____

_____

Reflection:
Take a moment to review your responses and consider any Consider how you can live out the reality of redemption in your daily life and share its message of hope with others.

WALKING IN LIGHT:
Navigating the Pathway to Salvation

"A man does not have to feel less than human to realise his sin; oppositely, he has to realise that he gets no special vindication for his sin." — Criss Jami, Killosophy

In the journey of life, amidst the twists and turns, highs, and lows, one quest remains paramount for humanity: the search for salvation. From the dawn of time, civilisations and individuals alike have sought answers to the profound questions of existence, purpose, and ultimate destiny. During this quest, the path to salvation stands as a beacon of hope, offering redemption, restoration, and reconciliation with God. Jesus is the exclusive path to salvation.

Are you craving something more profound in life, a hunger that goes beyond the physical? Is there an unquenchable longing within you to be delivered from sin? If so, Jesus offers the way! He proclaimed, "I am the bread of life. Whoever comes to me will never go hungry, and whoever believes in me will never be thirsty" (John 6:35).

Have you ever felt bewildered or adrift without purpose? Does it seem like darkness has enveloped your path, leaving you groping for direction? If so, Jesus is the path to salvation! He declared, "I am the light of the world. Whoever follows me will never walk in darkness but will have the light of life" (John 8:12).

Do you find yourself locked out of a fulfilling existence, trying numerous doors only to discover emptiness? If you seek entry into a truly meaningful life, Jesus is the way to salvation! He said, "I am the gate; whoever enters through me will be saved. They will come in and go out and find pasture" (John 10:9).

Have disappointments in people left you feeling betrayed? Are your relationships shallow and unfulfilling? If so, Jesus is the answer! He stated, "I am the good shepherd. The good shepherd lays down His life for the sheep. I am the good shepherd; I know my sheep and my sheep know me" (John 10:11, 14).

Do you ponder life beyond this world, tired of chasing things that perish? Do you question life's meaning and yearn for existence beyond death? If so, Jesus is the path to salvation! He declared, "I am the resurrection and the life. The one who believes in me will live, even though they die; and whoever lives by believing in me will never die" (John 11:25-26).

Jesus proclaimed, "I am the way and the truth and the life. No one comes to the Father except through me" (John 14:6).

Jesus is exclusive path to God. He is the complete means of reconciliation of believers with God. Jesus describes Himself as "the way," suggesting that He is the path that leads to God, calling for obedience to His teachings, imitation of His character, and reliance on His grace for salvation. Just as a map guides us on a journey, Jesus leads us to the Father, offering us direction, purpose, and ultimate fulfilment. Following Jesus involves surrendering our own ways and embracing His teachings, His example, and His lordship over our lives.

Jesus also identifies Himself as "the truth," implying that He embodies divine truth and reveals God's character and will to humanity. Jesus is the ultimate source of truth. Knowing and embracing Him leads to spiritual enlightenment and understanding. In a world of uncertainty and falsehood, Jesus embodies truth. Through His life, teachings, death, and resurrection, Jesus reveals the character and will of God to humanity. Accepting Jesus as "the truth" means aligning our beliefs, values, and actions with the truth He personifies.

By proclaiming Himself as "the life," Jesus emphasises that He offers abundant and eternal life to those who believe in Him. A choice to reject or ignore Him yields eternal separation from God. Jesus offers us not just existence but abundant and eternal life. Apart from Him, we are spiritually dead, separated from God and His purpose for our lives. Through faith in Jesus, we experience spiritual rebirth, restoration, and the promise of everlasting life in communion with God.

That hunger or emptiness you feel can only be satisfied by Jesus.

"Blessed are those who hunger and thirst for righteousness, for they will be filled" (Matthew 5:6). Jesus uses this powerful imagery of hunger and thirst to convey a deep longing and desire. Just as physical hunger and thirst drive us to seek sustenance, spiritual hunger and thirst compel us to seek righteousness. It is a recognition of our innate need for righteousness and a yearning for God's justice, goodness, and holiness to be manifested in our lives and in the world. The beatitude challenges us to examine our priorities and desires, asking ourselves what we truly hunger and thirst for in life. It calls us to cultivate a passionate pursuit of righteousness, seeking first the kingdom of God and His righteousness above all else (Matthew 6:33).

Christ dispels darkness, opens the door to a satisfying life, and offers friendship and guidance. Jesus is life—here and beyond. He is the way to salvation!

The exclusivity of salvation through Jesus challenges us to confront the relativism of our culture and boldly proclaim the truth of the Gospel. It compels us to prioritise our relationship with Jesus above all else, recognising Him as the ultimate authority in our lives. It motivates us to share the message of salvation with others, extending the invitation to all to come to know Jesus as the way, the truth, and the life.

The reason for your hunger, your sense of being lost, and the lack of meaning is the separation from God. The Bible teaches that our sin separates us from God (Romans 3:23). The void you feel is the absence of God in your life. We were created for a relationship with God, but sin severed that connection. Moreover, our sin leads to eternal separation from God in this life and the next (Romans 6:23).

How can this be resolved? Jesus is the answer! He took on our sin (2 Corinthians 5:21), died in our place (Romans 5:8), and triumphed over sin and death through His resurrection (Romans 6:4-5).

He did all of this because of His unconditional Love.

"Greater love has no one than this: to lay down one's life for one's friends" (John 15:13).

By placing our faith in Jesus and trusting His death as payment for our sins, all our sins are forgiven. Spiritual hunger is satisfied, lights shine, and a fulfilling life becomes accessible. We gain a true friend and shepherd and assurance of life after death—a resurrected life in eternal union with Jesus in heaven!

"For God so loved the world that he gave his one and only Son, that whoever believes in Him shall not perish but have eternal life" (John 3:16).

In 2004, as a young boy striving to find purpose in the world, I found myself grappling with feelings of emptiness and insignificance. One evening, while spending time at our usual meeting spot, I noticed a familiar friend heading towards what appeared to be a church gathering. His attire and the heartfelt melody of the hymn "No Never Alone" resonated deeply with me. Fearing the potential loss of yet another friend to the faith in Jesus Christ that everyone seemed to be talking about, I attempted to dissuade him, urging him to consider the opportunities of youth and the prospects of the future. Despite my efforts, Pindy remained steadfast, continuing to sing the hymn with unwavering devotion. Determined not to give up, I persisted in provoking him until we arrived at the church. To my astonishment, the congregation was echoing the same hymn Pindy had been singing earlier. Overwhelmed by the realisation that a God could love me so profoundly, sacrificing Himself for my salvation and offering fellowship with Him, I surrendered my life to Him without hesitation. Since then, my life has been a fulfilled one, impacting communities and serving the Lord. You too can obtain this hope by accepting Jesus as your Lord and Saviour.

Dear reader,

May your steps be guided by the light of God's love, leading you closer to Him with each stride. As you navigate this pathway, may you find strength in His promises and joy in His presence. Let your heart be open to His guidance, and may your journey be filled with blessings beyond measure.

Navigating the Pathway to Salvation - Reflective Activity

Objective: This activity aims to encourage personal reflection on the journey of navigating the pathway to salvation.

Instructions:

- Reflect on each question provided below.
- In your notebook, write down your thoughts, feelings, and any insights that come to mind.
- Take your time and be honest with yourself as you engage in this reflective process.
- After completing the activity, consider discussing your responses with a friend, mentor, or spiritual advisor for further insight and support.

Activity Questions:

1. What does salvation mean to you personally, and why is it important in your spiritual journey?

_____

_____

_____

Reflection:
Reflect on the significance of salvation in your life and how you can continue to walk confidently on the pathway to salvation with faith and trust in God's guidance.

GOD'S REDEMPTION BLUEPRINT:
Understanding the Plan of Salvation

The salvation of a single soul is more important than the production or preservation of all the epics and tragedies in the world. - C. S. Lewis

Salvation is liberation, a concept embraced across various world religions. Yet, each religion diverges on what deliverance entails, why it's necessary, and how one can attain it. The Bible, however, emphasises a singular plan for salvation. The crucial aspect of this plan is its divine origin—it's God's design, not humanity's. Human ideas of salvation might involve adhering to rituals, obeying commands, or seeking spiritual enlightenment. However, these notions aren't part of God's intended path to salvation.

God's Plan of Salvation-The Why in God's Blueprint

The fundamental understanding for God's intent revolves around why salvation is imperative. God's plan of salvation is a demonstration of His boundless love and mercy towards humanity. From the beginning of time, God's desire has been to reconcile sinful humanity to Himself and restore the broken relationship caused by sin. This plan was fulfilled through the sacrificial death and resurrection of Jesus Christ, His Son. Through Jesus, God provided the ultimate solution for sin and offered the gift of salvation to all who would believe in Him. God's plan of salvation is a testament to His faithfulness, grace, and compassion, as He offers forgiveness, redemption, and eternal life to those who repent and place their faith in Jesus Christ. It is a plan rooted in love, extending an invitation to every person to come into a life-transforming relationship with their Creator and experience the fullness of His salvation.

Why Do We Need Salvation?
Put simply, we require salvation because of our wrongdoing—our sin. The Bible asserts that everyone has sinned (Ecclesiastes 7:20; Romans 3:23; 1 John 1:8). Sin is rebellion against God, causing harm to others, self-damage, and, most significantly, dishonour to God. Moreover, due to God's holiness and justice, sin cannot go unpunished. The consequence of sin is death (Romans 6:23) and eternal separation from God (Revelation 20:11–15). Without God's plan of salvation, every human face eternal death.

God's Plan of Salvation – The What in God's Design
He alone provides salvation. Our sin and its consequences render us incapable of self-rescue. God incarnated as a human in Jesus Christ (John 1:1, 14) led a sinless life (2 Corinthians 5:21; Hebrews 4:15; 1 John 3:5) and offered Himself as a

flawless sacrifice on our behalf (1 Corinthians 15:3; Colossians 1:22; Hebrews 10:10). Being God, Jesus' death held immeasurable and eternal significance. His crucifixion fully atoned for the world's sins (1 John 2:2). His resurrection affirmed the sufficiency of His sacrifice and the accessibility of salvation.

God's Plan of Salvation – The How

In Acts 16:31, Paul was asked how to attain salvation. His reply: "Believe in the Lord Jesus Christ, and you will be saved." The path in God's plan of salvation is belief—this is the sole requirement (John 3:16; Ephesians 2:8–9). God has facilitated our salvation through Jesus Christ. All that's needed is to receive it through faith, entrusting solely in Jesus as Saviour (John 14:6; Acts 4:12).

Will You Accept God's Plan of Salvation?

If you're prepared to embrace God's plan of salvation, place your faith in Jesus as your Saviour. Change your mindset from embracing sin and rejecting God to renouncing sin and embracing God through Jesus Christ. Trust wholeheartedly in Jesus' sacrifice as the complete payment for your sins. By doing so, God's Word assures that you'll be saved, your sins forgiven, and you'll spend eternity in heaven. There's no decision more crucial than to place your faith in Jesus Christ as your Saviour today!

To begin journey, pray this simple salvatory prayer:

"*Heavenly Father,*

I come before you acknowledging that I am a sinner in need of your forgiveness. I believe that Jesus Christ died for my sins and rose again, and I accept Him as my Lord and Savior.

Please forgive me of my sins, come into my heart, and guide me in your ways. Thank you for your love and grace.

In Jesus' name, Amen."

Dear reader,
If you pray and sincerely believe these words, you have taken your first step towards salvation and a renewed relationship with God. Remember, it's not just the words themselves but the sincerity and faith behind them that matters most.

Understanding the Plan of Salvation - Reflective Activity

Objective: This activity aims to encourage personal reflection on the concept of the plan of salvation.

Instructions:

- Reflect on each question provided below.
- Write down your thoughts, feelings, and any insights that come to mind.
- Take your time and be honest with yourself as you engage in this reflective process.
- After completing the activity, consider discussing your responses with a friend, mentor, or spiritual advisor for further insight and support.

Activity Questions:

1. How does the assurance of God's love, grace, and redemption through Jesus Christ impact your beliefs, values, and relationship with God?

_____

_____

_____

Reflection:

Take a moment to analyse the implications of the plan of salvation for your faith journey and how you can continue to embrace its truth and promise in your daily life.

A BRIDGE TO REDEMPTION:
Embracing Salvation through Faith

"The recognition of sin is the beginning of salvation." - Martin Luther

How Can I be Saved?
The fundamental question of **"How can I be saved?"** encompasses our eternal destiny, making it the most significant query we face. Fortunately, the Bible provides clear guidance on achieving salvation. When the Philippian jailer sought answers from Paul and Silas, they responded unequivocally: "Believe in the Lord Jesus, and you will be saved" (Acts 16:31). To be saved, one must first recognise his/her need for salvation. This begins with acknowledging that all have sinned and fallen short of God's standard (Romans 3:23). Next, one must believe in Jesus Christ as the Son of God who died on the cross for the forgiveness of sins and rose again, conquering death (John 3:16, Romans 10:9).

Salvation is received through faith in Jesus Christ alone, not by our own works or efforts (Ephesians 2:8-9). Therefore, to be saved, one must repent of his/her sins, turning away from a life lived apart from God, and turn to Jesus Christ in faith, surrendering his/her life to Him as Lord and Saviour (Acts 2:38, Acts 16:31).

Salvation is a free gift from God, offered to all who believe and receive Jesus Christ into their hearts. Through faith in Jesus, one is reconciled to God, adopted into His family, and assured of eternal life with Him (John 1:12, Romans 5:1, 1 John 5:11-13).

To fully grasp the answer to the question, **how I can be saved**, we must pursue answers for the following:
- Why do I need to be saved?
- What am I saved from?

Why Do I Need to Be Saved?
Sin taints us all (Romans 3:23). It's inherent from birth (Psalm 51:5), and our choices further perpetuate it (Ecclesiastes 7:20; 1 John 1:8). Sin separates us from God, steering us toward eternal ruin. The need for salvation arises from the reality of sin and its consequences. As human beings, we are inherently flawed and fall short of God's perfect standard (Romans 3:23). Sin separates us from God, our Creator, and leads to spiritual death (Romans 6:23). Without salvation, we are unable to bridge the gap between ourselves and God or to attain the righteousness necessary to enter His presence (Isaiah 59:2). Furthermore, the consequences of sin extend beyond this life to eternity,

resulting in eternal separation from God in a place of punishment called hell (Revelation 20:15). Therefore, the need for salvation is essential for every individual to experience reconciliation with God, receive forgiveness for sins, and inherit the gift of eternal life (John 3:16, Ephesians 2:8-9). Salvation offers hope, redemption, and the promise of a restored relationship with God, making it indispensable for all who seek true fulfilment and meaning in life. Our sin warrants death (Romans 6:23). Beyond physical demise, sin is an affront to an eternal God (Psalm 51:4), demanding an eternal penalty which is eternal destruction (Matthew 25:46; Revelation 20:15).

What Am I Being Saved From?

Believers are saved from the consequences of sin and the brokenness it brings to their relationship with God. Sin separates humanity from God, leading to spiritual death and eternal separation from His presence. Through Jesus Christ, believers are saved from this separation and granted eternal life with God. They are rescued from the bondage of sin, the guilt and shame it brings, and the ultimate judgment it incurs. Salvation brings reconciliation with God, restoring the broken relationship and offering forgiveness, grace, and the promise of eternal life. It's a transformational journey from darkness to light, from condemnation to redemption, made possible through the sacrificial love of Jesus Christ.

How Did God Provide Salvation?

Given sin's eternal penalty, only God, infinite and eternal, could settle it. God, manifest as Jesus Christ, assumed human form, dwelt among us, and imparted teachings. Upon rejection and facing death, He willingly sacrificed Himself, crucified for us (John 10:15). As both human and God, Jesus' death held infinite value, fully paying for our sin (1 John 2:2). His resurrection confirmed the sufficiency of His sacrifice.

What Do I Need to Do?

"Believe in the Lord Jesus, and you will be saved" (Acts 16:31). God accomplished the work; our role is to receive His offered salvation in faith (Ephesians 2:8-9). Place unwavering trust in Jesus as the atonement for your sins. Embrace Him, and eternal peril will be averted (John 3:16). Salvation is a gift awaiting your acceptance. Jesus embodies the path to salvation (John 14:6).

Dear reader,

Have you embraced this designed route to achieve salvation with God?

Embracing Salvation through Faith - Reflective Activity

Objective: This activity aims to encourage personal reflection on the concept of embracing salvation through faith.

Instructions:

- Reflect on each question provided below.
- Write down your thoughts, feelings, and any insights that come to mind.
- After completing the activity, consider discussing your responses with a friend, mentor, or spiritual advisor for further insight and support.

Activity Questions:

1. How do you define faith in the context of salvation? What role does faith play in the journey of embracing salvation, and how does it influence your relationship with God?

_____

_____

_____

Reflection:
Take some time to reflect on the significance of faith in your life and how you can continue to nurture and strengthen your faith journey as you embrace salvation through faith in Jesus Christ.

THE URGENCY OF REDEMPTION:

Understanding The Need to Be Saved

"The need to be saved is not just about escaping punishment; it's about finding freedom from sin's grip, restoration of brokenness, and eternal fellowship with a loving God."- Nicholas Robertson

The urgency of salvation lies in its eternal implications. Every moment without salvation is a risk of separation from God and His ultimate plan for our lives. Tomorrow is never guaranteed, and the uncertainty of life stresses the importance of making a decision for salvation today. In light of the brevity of life and the uncertainty of what lies beyond, embracing salvation becomes not just a priority, but an urgent necessity. It's a call to seize the opportunity for reconciliation with God, to find peace, purpose, and eternal security in Him before it's too late.

The urgency of salvation is indeed reflected in the message of Acts 16:31, where Paul and Silas urged the jailer to believe in the Lord Jesus for salvation. Their words emphasize not only the simplicity of salvation through faith in Jesus but also the immediacy with which one should embrace it. This urgency stems from the understanding that salvation is a matter of eternal significance, and delaying acceptance of it only prolongs the risk of spiritual separation from God. Just as the jailer was urged to believe and be saved without delay, so too are all who hear the message of salvation called to respond swiftly and decisively.

The Bible emphasizes the reasons for salvation, each highlighting its urgency in different ways.

- **We need Salvation as we are entirely Ensnared in Sin**

It's not about self-rescue, which we cannot achieve, but the necessity of being saved. The Bible highlights the complete corruption of humanity by sin. "There is no one righteous, not even one... no one who does good, not even one" (Romans 3:10–12). We need the Good Shepherd to seek out the lost and joyfully bring them home (see Luke 15:3–6).

- **We need Salvation as we're Subject to God's Wrath**

By nature, we're deserving of divine wrath (Ephesians 2:3). Without salvation, we're condemned: "Whoever does not believe stands condemned already..." (John 3:18). Jesus Christ, the Righteous One, is needed to appease God's wrath and take our judgment.

- **Salvation is necessary since we face the danger of Hell**

After death comes judgment (Hebrews 9:27), and without God's salvation, we risk a fate like the tormented rich man in

Hades (Luke 16:23). We require a Saviour to rescue us from a fate worse than death.

- **We need Salvation because we're Spiritually Lifeless**

Prior to salvation, we're "dead in [our] sins" (Colossians 2:13). The dead cannot help themselves; we need resurrection. We require Christ's life-giving power, the only force that can overcome death.

- **Our Hearts are hardened by Evil**

"The heart is deceitful... beyond cure" (Jeremiah 17:9). The unsaved are "darkened in their understanding" and separated from God's life due to hardened hearts (Ephesians 4:18). We necessitate a supernatural work of the Holy Spirit to transform our hearts and align them with God's will.

- **We're enslaved to sin and Satan and need Liberation**

"All are under the power of sin" (Romans 3:9). In our natural state, we're ensnared by Satan and bound by his will (2 Timothy 2:26). We require a Redeemer to set us free from sin's grip (Romans 6:18).

- **Conflict with God is a Stark Reality**

"The mind governed by the flesh is hostile to God" (Romans 8:7–8). We need Jesus, the Prince of Peace, to reconcile us with God and welcome us into His family as adopted children.

When Jesus instructed Nicodemus, "You must be born again," it spoke to an imperative necessity and urgency (John 3:7). Salvation, receiving this new birth, isn't merely an idea or suggestion—it's the deepest requirement of the human soul: "You must be born again." Salvation is urgent and essential. The brevity of life, the consequences of sin, and the promise of eternal life all converge to accentuate the paramount importance of embracing salvation without delay. Today, as in every age, the call to believe in the Lord Jesus Christ and be saved echoes with urgency, inviting all to experience the transformative power of God's grace and the assurance of eternal life in Him.

Dear reader,
Have you accepted the Lord Jesus Christ as your saviour. If yes, have you been sharing this message with profound urgency?

Understanding the Need to Be Saved - Reflective Activity

Objective: This activity aims to encourage personal reflection on the importance of acknowledging the need for salvation.

Instructions:

- Reflect on each question provided below.
- Write down your thoughts, feelings, and any insights that come to mind.
- Take your time and be honest with yourself as you engage in this reflective process.
- After completing the activity, consider discussing your responses with a friend, mentor, or spiritual advisor for further insight and support.

Activity Question:

1. How does acknowledging your need for salvation align with your understanding of God's love and mercy, and how does it shape your relationship with Him?

_____

_____

_____

Reflection:
Consider how you can deepen your appreciation of God's grace and share the message of salvation with others.

THE WAY OF REDEMPTION:
What Are the Steps to Salvation?

"There is no other salvation except that which begins and ends with grace." - Charles Spurgeon

Numerous individuals are in pursuit of a definitive route to salvation, yearning for a systematic method to ensure deliverance. They seek a guidebook with exact instructions that guarantee a path to be saved. Various faiths endeavour to impart to their adherents diverse methods to achieve salvation:

- Islam offers its Five Pillars, suggesting that adhering to these pillars guarantees salvation.
- Roman Catholicism introduces seven sacraments.
- Various Christian denominations add additional acts like baptism, public confession, repentance, and speaking in tongues as essential steps toward salvation.

However, the Bible presents a different perspective, outlining just one step to salvation. When the Philippian jailer asked Paul about being saved, the answer was straightforward: **"Believe in the Lord Jesus Christ, and you will be saved"** (Acts 16:30-31). Faith in Jesus Christ stands as the sole "step" toward salvation.

The Bible's message is clear: all of us have fallen short in our relationship with God (Romans 3:23), resulting in the deserved punishment of eternal separation (Romans 6:23). Yet, driven by boundless love (John 3:16), God took on human form, bearing the weight of our penalty (Romans 5:8; 2 Corinthians 5:21). For all who embrace Jesus Christ through grace and faith, God promises forgiveness and eternal life (John 1:12; 3:16; 5:24; Acts 16:31).

Salvation isn't about fulfilling a checklist to earn favour. Baptism, confession, repentance, and obedience to God are outcomes of salvation—they aren't steps leading to it. Our sin prevents us from earning salvation; even if we follow a thousand steps, it wouldn't be enough. This is precisely why Jesus sacrificed Himself for us. We're powerless to settle our debt or cleanse ourselves from sin. Only God could achieve our salvation, extending it to all who accept it.

Salvation and absolution don't rely on following specific steps; it's about recognising Christ as our Saviour and acknowledging His completed work. God asks for one step—accepting Jesus as our Saviour, trusting Him completely for salvation. This sets Christianity apart—it doesn't offer a checklist. Instead, it acknowledges God's finished work and invites the repentant to embrace Him in faith.

Dear reader,

Have you accepted this priceless gift of salvation and are you fervently spreading the message to others?

Steps to Salvation - Reflective Activity

Objective: This activity aims to encourage personal reflection on the steps involved in the process of salvation.

Instructions:

- Reflect on each question provided below.
- Write down your thoughts, feelings, and any insights that come to mind.
- Take your time and be honest with yourself as you engage in this reflective process.
- After completing the activity, consider discussing your responses with a friend, mentor, or spiritual advisor for further insight and support.

Activity Question:

1. What specific actions or decisions do you believe are necessary for someone to experience salvation, and why are these steps important in your faith journey?

_____

_____

_____

Reflection:

Take a moment to reflect on the significance of the steps to salvation in your life and how they continue to shape your faith journey.

THE GOOD NEWS UNVEILED:
Understanding the Gospel

"The gospel is not a doctrine of the tongue, but of life. It cannot be grasped by reason and memory only, but it is fully understood when it possesses the whole soul and penetrates to the inner recesses of the heart." — John Calvin

The term "gospel" translates to "good news" and appears 93 times in the Bible, exclusively in the New Testament. In Greek, it originates from the word "euaggelion," forming the basis for English words like evangelist, evangel, and evangelical. Broadly speaking, the gospel encompasses the entirety of Scripture. Yet, more specifically, it refers to the joyous tidings concerning Christ and the pathway to salvation.

Understanding the gospel hinges on comprehending why it's considered good news. To grasp its goodness, one must first recognise the bad news. The Old Testament Law, introduced during Moses's time to Israel (Deuteronomy 5:1), acts as a standard by which sin is measured. Anything falling short of this "perfect" benchmark represents sin. The Law's righteous demands are so stringent that no human could fulfil them entirely—neither in the letter nor in the spirit. Regardless of our perceived goodness or badness, we all share the same spiritual condition—we've sinned, and the consequence of sin is death, entailing separation from God, the source of life (Romans 3:23). For us to enter heaven, God's abode, the realm of life and light, sin must be either eradicated or atoned for. The Law emphasises that cleansing from sin necessitates the sacrificial shedding of innocent blood (Hebrews 9:22). The gospel revolves around Jesus' crucifixion as the ultimate sacrifice, fulfilling the Law's righteous standards (Romans 8:3–4; Hebrews 10:5–10). In the context of the Law, animal sacrifices were offered repeatedly, symbolising sin, and pointing to Christ's impending sacrifice (Hebrews 10:3–4). When Christ offered Himself at Calvary, this symbol transformed into a reality for all who believe (Hebrews 10:11–18). The work of atonement is now complete, and that is indeed great news.

The gospel also involves Jesus' resurrection on the third day. "He was delivered over to death for our sins and was raised to life for our justification" (Romans 4:25). The fact that Jesus triumphed over sin and death (the penalty for sin) is indeed good news. More significantly, He extends this victory to us (John 14:19). The elements of the gospel are explicitly detailed in 1 Corinthians 15:3–6, a pivotal passage concerning God's joyful news: "For what I received I passed on to you as of first importance: that Christ died for our sins according to the Scriptures, that He was buried, that He was raised on the third day according to the Scriptures, and that He appeared to Cephas, and then to the Twelve. After that, He appeared to more than five hundred of the brothers and sisters at the same time, most of whom are still living."

Firstly, note that Paul "received" and "passed on" the gospel; it's a divine message, not a human invention. Secondly, the gospel is "of first importance." Whenever the apostles preached, they emphasised Christ's crucifixion and resurrection. Thirdly, the gospel is substantiated by evidence: Christ died for our sins (confirmed by His burial), and He rose on the third day (verified by eyewitnesses). Lastly, all of this was in fulfilment of Scripture—the overarching theme of the Bible is humanity's salvation through Christ. The Bible itself is the gospel.

The gospel is a bold message, and we proudly proclaim it. It carries power because it's God's good news. "I am not ashamed of the gospel, because it is the power of God that brings salvation to everyone who believes: first to the Jew, then to the Gentile" (Romans 1:16). It brings salvation, a transformation to the human heart. It's universal, meant for both Jews and Gentiles, and it's received through faith; salvation is a gift from God (Ephesians 2:8–9).

The gospel reveals that God's love for the world led Him to offer His only Son to die for our sins (John 3:16). It guarantees our salvation, eternal life, and a heavenly home through Christ (John 14:1–4). "He has given us new birth into a living hope through the resurrection of Jesus Christ from the dead, and into an inheritance that can never perish, spoil, or fade. This inheritance is kept in heaven for you" (1 Peter 1:3–4).

Understanding the gospel means acknowledging that we cannot earn our salvation; redemption and justification were completed on the cross (John 19:30). Jesus is the atoning sacrifice for our sins (1 John 2:2). The gospel reveals that, once enemies of God, we are now reconciled by Christ's blood and adopted into God's family (Romans 5:10; John 1:12). "See what great love the Father has lavished on us, that we should be called children of God! And that is what we are!" (1 John 3:1).

The gospel declares that "there is now no condemnation for those who are in Christ Jesus" (Romans 8:1). Rejecting the gospel is embracing the bad news. Condemnation results from not believing in the Son of God, the sole means of salvation provided by God. "For God did not send his Son into the world to condemn the world, but to save the world through Him. Whoever believes in Him is not condemned, but whoever does not believe stands condemned already because they have not believed in the name of God's one and only Son" (John 3:17–18). In a world destined for doom, **God offers the Gospel of Jesus Christ as great news!**

Dear reader,

Having encountered salvation, we must become bearers of this message of hope. What are someways you can effectively convey the gospel?

Understanding the Gospel - Reflective Activity

Objective: This activity aims to encourage personal reflection on the message and significance of the gospel.

Instructions:

- Reflect on each question provided below.
- Write down your thoughts, feelings, and any insights that come to mind.
- Take your time and be honest with yourself as you engage in this reflective process.
- After completing the activity, consider discussing your responses with a friend, mentor, or spiritual advisor for further insight and support.

Activity Questions:

1. Reflect on your understanding of the gospel. What does the gospel mean to you personally, and why do you believe it is important in your spiritual journey?

_____

_____

_____

Reflection:
Consider how you can deepen your understanding of the gospel and share its message of hope and redemption with others.

UNRAVELLING THE MYSTERY:
Examining the Concept of Sin

"Our sin is what separates us from God, but it's our self-righteousness that keeps us from running to Him for the grace He willingly gives to all who come." - Paul David Tripp

What is Sin?

The Bible portrays sin as a violation of God's law (1 John 3:4) and an act of defiance against Him (Deuteronomy 9:7, Joshua 1:18). Sin is not just breaking a moral code or committing wrongful acts; it is what amounts to a fundamental separation from God, the source of all goodness and righteousness. The term "sin" originates from the Greek word "Hamartia," which translates to "to miss the mark or to err." To sin is to deviate or stray from the path of righteousness and integrity, to err or go astray. It involves transgressing the law of God, violating His commands, and committing acts contrary to His will. Sin encompasses wrongful deeds, offenses, and violations of divine law, whether in thought or action. Sin permeates every aspect of our lives, tarnishing our thoughts, words, and actions. It distorts our relationships, both with God and with one another, leading to brokenness and pain. Its origins trace back to Lucifer, an exalted angel who aspired to surpass God and thus succumbed to downfall (Isaiah 14:12-15). Renamed Satan, he introduced sin to humanity by tempting Adam and Eve with the allure of becoming like God, initiating rebellion in the Garden of Eden (Genesis 3).

There are different categories of sin: Inherited, imputed and personal sin.

- **Inherited Sin**

The consequences of Adam's disobedience permeate humanity, and we, as his descendants, have inherited sin from him. Scripture explains that sin entered the world through Adam, leading to spiritual death, and consequently, all people bear the imprint of sin (Romans 5:12). This inherited depravity is known as original sin, akin to inheriting physical traits from parents (Psalm 51:5).

- **Imputed Sin**

Imputed sin, another form, stems from Adam's guilt being attributed to us (Romans 5:18). It implies that we are held accountable for Adam's transgression. This imputation brought death to all, even before the Mosaic Law, affecting our standing before God. However, God employed imputation for humanity's benefit by imputing believers' sin to Jesus Christ. He, though sinless, bore the penalty of sin on the cross, representing the sins of the world (1 John 2:2).

Simultaneously, God imputed Christ's righteousness to believers, crediting their accounts with His purity (2 Corinthians 5:21).

- **Personal Sin**

Personal sin, the third type, characterises daily transgressions committed by every individual due to the inherited sin nature. Untruths, even murder, fall under this category. Those who haven't embraced faith in Jesus Christ are liable for these personal sins and the broader effects of sin. Conversely, believers are freed from the eternal penalty of sin through Christ and empowered by the Holy Spirit to resist sin.

How to be delivered from Sin?

Confession of personal sins leads to restoration of fellowship with God, as He forgives and cleanses believers (1 John 1:9). Humanity stands thrice condemned due to inherited, imputed, and personal sin, deserving death as a penalty (Romans 6:23; Revelation 20:11-15). However, through faith in Jesus Christ, sin's consequences were crucified on the cross, providing redemption and forgiveness through His sacrifice (Ephesians 1:7).

Dear reader,

You can be saved from your sins. Repent and be saved.

Examining the Concept of Sin - Reflective Activity

Objective: This activity aims to encourage personal reflection on the concept of sin and its implications in one's life.

Instructions:

- Reflect on each question provided below.
- Write down your thoughts, feelings, and any insights that come to mind.
- Take your time and be honest with yourself as you engage in this reflective process.
- After completing the activity, consider discussing your responses with a friend, mentor, or spiritual advisor for further insight and support.

Activity Question:

1. What does sin mean to you personally, and how do you perceive its impact on your life and relationships?

_____

_____

_____

Reflection:
Consider how you can deepen your understanding of sin and its consequences, and how you can strive to live a life aligned with God's will.

THE ULTIMATE SACRIFICE:
Exploring the Necessity of Jesus' Death

"While sin is overflowing, [grace] pour itself forth so exuberantly, that it not only overcomes the flood of sin, but wholly absorbs it." - John Calvin

Why did Jesus have to die?

When pondering the question: **"Why did Jesus have to die?"** it's crucial not to cast doubt on God and His chosen method to redeem humanity. Questioning if there could have been "another way" implies that God's chosen path isn't optimal and that an alternative method might be better. Typically, what we deem a "better" approach is what aligns with our own understanding. But before grappling with anything God does, it's essential to recognise that His ways are not our ways—His thoughts are loftier than ours (Isaiah 55:8). Additionally, Deuteronomy 32:4 emphasises that "He is the Rock, His works are perfect, and all His ways are just. A faithful God who does no wrong, upright, and just is He." Hence, His devised plan of salvation is faultless, just, and righteous, beyond any humanly devised improvement. The Scriptures declare, "For I delivered to you as of first importance what I also received: that Christ died for our sins in accordance with the Scriptures, that He was buried, that

He was raised on the third day in accordance with the Scriptures" (1 Corinthians 15:3-4). The evidence confirms Jesus, though sinless, bled, and died on the cross. Most importantly, the Bible clarifies why Jesus' death and resurrection form ***the sole gateway to heaven***.

Additionally, I have composed some other justification for the necessity of Christ's death:

- **Jesus' Death was the Penalty for Sin**

Sin must be punished by death as explained in Romans 6:23. God initially fashioned humans flawlessly. However, when Adam and Eve disobeyed God's commands, He had to administer punishment. A just judge cannot pardon lawbreakers. Similarly, ignoring sin would compromise God's righteousness. Death becomes God's justified consequence for sin. "For the wages of sin is death" (Romans 6:23). Even exemplary deeds cannot offset offenses against the holy God. Compared to His righteousness, "All our righteousness are as filthy rags" (Isaiah 64:6b). Since Adam's transgression, every individual has flouted God's righteous decrees. "For all have sinned and fall short of the glory of God" (Romans 3:23). Sin encompasses not just significant transgressions like murder or blasphemy but also inclines toward the love of money, hatred for enemies, deceitful tongues, and pride. Due to sin, everyone stands deserving of death—a perpetual separation from God in hell.

- **The Covenant necessitated an Innocent Death.**

Although God exiled Adam and Eve from the garden, He didn't abandon them without the hope of reconciliation. He pledged to send a Saviour to defeat the serpent (Genesis 3:15). Until then, people would offer innocent lambs as a sign of repentance from sin and faith in the future Sacrifice from God who would bear their penalty. God reiterated His commitment to the Sacrifice through figures like Abraham and Moses. Herein lies the brilliance of God's immaculate plan: God Himself furnished the only sacrifice (Jesus) capable of atoning for the sins of His people. God's perfect Son fulfilled God's perfect law requirement flawlessly. It's a perfectly ingenious plan in its simplicity. "God made Him (Christ), who knew no sin, to be sin for us that we might become the righteousness of God in Him" (2 Corinthians 5:21).

- **The Prophets Predicted Jesus' Death**

From Adam to Jesus, God dispatched prophets to warn humanity of sin's consequences and foretell the advent of the Messiah. One prophet, Isaiah, envisioned Him: "Who has believed what they heard from us? And to whom has the arm of the LORD been revealed? For He grew up before Him like a young plant, and like a root out of dry ground; He had no form or majesty that we should look at Him, and no beauty that we should desire Him. He was despised and rejected by men; a man of sorrows and acquainted with grief; and as one from whom men hide their faces He was despised, and we esteemed Him not. Surely, He has borne our griefs and carried our sorrows; yet we esteemed Him stricken, smitten by God, and afflicted. But He was wounded for our transgressions; He was crushed for our iniquities; upon Him was the chastisement that brought us peace, and with His stripes we are healed. All we like sheep have gone astray; we have turned everyone to his own way; and the LORD has laid on Him the iniquity of us all. He was oppressed, and He was afflicted, yet He opened not his mouth; like a lamb that is led to the slaughter, and like a sheep that before its shearers is silent, so He opened not His mouth. By oppression and judgment, He was taken away; and as for His generation, who considered that He was cut off out of the land of the living, stricken for the transgression of my people? And they made His grave with the wicked and with a rich man in His death, although He had done no violence, and there was no deceit in His mouth. Yet it was the will of the LORD to crush Him; He has put Him to grief; when His soul makes an offering for sin, He shall see His offspring; He shall prolong His days; the will of the LORD shall prosper in His hand. Out of the anguish of His soul He shall see and be satisfied; by His knowledge shall the righteous one, my servant, make many to be accounted righteous, and He shall bear their iniquities. Therefore, I will divide Him a portion with the many, and He shall divide the spoil with the strong, because He poured out His soul to death and was numbered with the transgressors; yet He bore the sin of many and makes intercession for the transgressors" (Isaiah 53:1-12). He likened the coming Sacrifice to a lamb slaughtered for the sins of others. Jesus' death on the cross was not a tragic accident or a cruel twist of fate; it was the culmination of God's redemptive plan for humanity.

- **Jesus' Death was a part of God's Redemptive Plan**

Sin had separated mankind from God, creating an unbridgeable chasm between His holiness and our fallen nature. The consequence of sin is death, both physical and spiritual, and without intervention, humanity was doomed to eternal separation from God. However, out of His unfathomable love for us, God sent His Son, Jesus Christ, to pay the price for our sins. By willingly laying down His life on the cross, Jesus took upon Himself the punishment that we rightfully deserved. His sacrificial death satisfied the demands of justice and opened the way for reconciliation between God and humanity. Through Jesus' death and resurrection, the power of sin and death was broken, and all who believe in Him can experience forgiveness, restoration, and eternal life. Thus, Jesus had to die to fulfil God's plan of salvation and to offer humanity the gift of redemption and eternal hope.

Dear reader,
Jesus' death was paramount to our salvation.

Exploring the Necessity of Jesus' Death - Reflective Activity

Objective: This activity aims to encourage personal reflection on the necessity and significance of Jesus' death.

Instructions:

- Reflect on each question provided below.
- Write down your thoughts, feelings, and any insights that come to mind.
- Take your time and be honest with yourself as you engage in this reflective process.
- After completing the activity, consider discussing your responses with a friend, mentor, or spiritual advisor for further insight and support.

Activity Questions:

1. What does Jesus' death mean to you personally, and why do you believe it was essential for humanity's salvation?

_____

_____

_____

Reflection:
Consider how you can deepen your appreciation of Jesus' sacrifice and share its message of hope and salvation with others.

TRIUMPH OVER DEATH:
Understanding the Significance of Jesus' Resurrection

"Jesus's resurrection is the beginning of God's new project not to snatch people away from earth to heaven but to colonise earth with the life of heaven. That, after all, is what the Lord's Prayer is about." — N.T. Wright

Jesus's resurrection holds numerous implications: Firstly, it serves as a testament to the immense power of God Himself. Belief in the resurrection is essentially belief in God. If God exists and holds authority over the universe, then He indeed possesses the power to resurrect the deceased. This power to reverse death's grasp, eliminating its sting, asserts God's sovereignty over life and death (1 Corinthians 15:54–55). By resurrecting Jesus, God reaffirms His absolute dominion over life's cycles.

Moreover, Jesus's resurrection validates His claims as the Son of God and Messiah. His resurrection stands as the celestial "sign" endorsing His ministry (Matthew 16:1–4). Supported by the testimony of numerous eyewitnesses (1 Corinthians 15:3–8), His resurrection serves as undeniable proof of His role as the world's Saviour.

Another critical aspect is how Jesus's resurrection attests to His sinless nature and divine essence. Foretold in Scriptures that the "Holy One" would never decay (Psalm 16:10), Jesus, even after His death, didn't undergo corruption (Acts 13:32–37). This formed the basis of Paul's teachings regarding the forgiveness of sins through Jesus (Acts 13:38–39).

Furthermore, Christ's resurrection substantiates the Old Testament prophecies about His suffering and revival (Acts 17:2–3). His resurrection stands as evidence supporting His predictions of rising on the third day (Mark 8:31; 9:31; 10:34). Without Christ's resurrection, our hope for salvation and eternal life would cease to exist, rendering our faith ineffective (1 Corinthians 15:14–19). Jesus's declaration, "I am the resurrection and the life" (John 11:25), asserts His role as the source of life itself. In Him lies not just life but the essence of life, transcending the power of death. Those who trust in Jesus receive His life, partaking in His victory over death (1 John 5:11–12). Death's defeat becomes inevitable (1 Corinthians 15:53–57).

Christ's resurrection is pivotal, not just for Himself but as a testament to the resurrection of humanity—an essential aspect of the Christian faith. Unlike other religions with mortal founders, Christianity, with Jesus transcending death, promises the same for His followers. His resurrection, assuring ours at His second coming, inspires triumphant faith (1 Corinthians 15:55). This monumental event affects our present service to the Lord. Paul encourages unwavering dedication to the Lord's work, knowing our labour holds eternal significance (1 Corinthians 15:58). Aware of our resurrection to new life, we can endure hardships, even as many martyrs in history, valuing eternal life over worldly existence.

Jesus's resurrection symbolises the victorious triumph for every believer. His death, burial, and resurrection according to Scriptures (1 Corinthians 15:3–4) affirm His imminent return. Believers, both deceased and alive at His coming, will receive transformed, glorified bodies (1 Thessalonians 4:13–18). The resurrection of Jesus Christ holds paramount importance, confirming His identity, validating His sacrifice, displaying God's power over death, and assuring eternal life for those who believe.

Dear reader,
Let His victory over death ignite hope within you and inspire a life of purpose and joy. As we celebrate His resurrection, may we walk boldly in the power of His triumph, knowing that in Him, we find ultimate victory over sin and death. Let His resurrection be not just a historical event but a living reality in our hearts, transforming us into vessels of His grace and love.

Reflecting on the Importance of Jesus' Resurrection

Objective: This activity encourages personal reflection on the importance of Jesus' resurrection.

Instructions:

- Reflect on each question provided below.
- Write down your thoughts, feelings, and any insights.
- Take your time and be honest as you engage in this process.
- After completing the activity, consider discussing your responses with someone for further insight.

Activity Questions:

1. Consider the significance of Jesus' resurrection. What does it mean to you personally, and why is it important in Christianity?

   _____

   _____

   _____

Reflection:
Reflect on the importance of Jesus' resurrection in your life and faith journey. Consider how you can deepen your understanding of this event and its implications for your spiritual growth.

RECOGNISING THE NEED:
Understanding Why I Need a Saviour

"Never does a person see any beauty in Christ as a Saviour, until they discover that they are a lost and ruined sinner." - J. C. Ryle

Humanity's need for a Saviour is a vast concept rooted in the nature of God and humanity. God is holy and humanity were sinful being's incapable of saving themselves. When we say, **"we need a Saviour,"** it universally includes every individual that has existed throughout history. All of humanity needs to be redeemed from sin. The term "saviour" in the Bible incorporates anyone delivering or rescuing others—such as Othniel and Ehud who were both designated as "saviours" (Judges 3:9, 15). God Himself is also termed "Saviour" (Isaiah 43:11; 45:21–22; 60:16). However, Jesus Christ is the one who could redeem humanity from its sinful state, becoming the bridge between sinful people and God. A loving God becoming the antidote for ridding humanity of the pain of sin, making it possible for us to fellowship with God again. "For this is how God loved the world: He gave His one and only Son, so that everyone who believes in Him will not perish but have eternal life. (John 3:16, NLT) The foundation of our need for a Saviour is rooted in God's plan for humanity and His absolute holiness, which cannot coexist with sin. Additionally, every human possesses an intrinsic sin nature and has committed sin, making perfection unattainable. Living in the presence of God demands sinless perfection, which none of us possess. Therefore, to accomplish His goals, God must address the human condition. This is why we need a Saviour—identified in Scripture as Jesus Christ. While we look forward with hope to that wonderful day when the glory of our great God and Saviour, Jesus Christ, will be revealed. He gave His life to free us from every kind of sin, to cleanse us, and to make us His very own people, totally committed to doing good deeds. (Titus 2:13–14).

Our need for Jesus, the Saviour, is imperative because we require sanctification: "without holiness, no one will see the Lord" (Hebrews 12:14). Jesus doesn't merely improve us; He transforms us into entirely new beings (2 Corinthians 5:17; Galatians 6:15). God's design for humanity aims to glorify Him and eternally commune with Him (Isaiah 43:7; Psalm 27:4). His desire is to shape us into the image of His Son (Romans 8:29). The Creator seeks relationships with beings created in His image (Genesis 1:27). Sin disrupted this relationship, necessitating a Saviour—God sent His only Son to prepare us for eternity and display His glory. The concept of God's holiness is emphasised over 900 times in the Bible. It's crucial to God's creation. Pursuing holiness is underscored (1 Peter 1:15). Recognising God's holiness is vital in approaching Him (Matthew 6:9). We need a Saviour because God is too pure to coexist with sin (Habakkuk 1:13).

In Romans 3:10–18, Paul underscores that every person has sinned (Romans 3:23). The Bible asserts that all need redemption; no one can cleanse their sins (Jeremiah 13:23; Romans 3:10; Psalm 14:1). Even those who deny their sinfulness are declared sinners (1 John 1:8). God has a perfect plan involving humanity, but our sinfulness hinders its execution. God's holiness requires cleansing, or eternal separation is inevitable. Thus, God's solution was to offer the perfect sacrifice—His Son on the cross—to cleanse and reconcile us to Himself. Our inability to save ourselves highlights our need for a Saviour. Without Christ, we are without hope and God (Ephesians 2:12). Thankfully, God provided Jesus as our Saviour, demonstrating His love and mercy. Through Jesus, justified by grace, we become heirs of eternal hope (Titus 3:7). Jesus' sacrifice exemplifies God's love and reveals the depth of our need for a Saviour. The cross stands as proof of our need for redemption.

We need a Saviour because, as human beings, we are inherently flawed and incapable of meeting God's perfect standard on our own (Romans 3:23). Despite our best efforts, we all fall short of God's righteousness due to the presence of sin in our lives. Sin separates us from God, our Creator, and leads to spiritual death. God loves you deeply and desires a relationship with you. That's why He sent Jesus Christ, His Son, to be your Saviour. Jesus lived a perfect and sinless life, died on the cross to pay the penalty for your sins, and rose again from the dead, conquering sin, and death once and for all (1 Corinthians 5:22). Through faith in Jesus Christ, you can experience forgiveness, reconciliation with God, and the gift of eternal life. Without a Saviour, you would be left to face the consequences of sin on your own. But with Jesus as your Saviour, you can receive salvation and find hope, purpose, and fulfilment in Him.

Dear reader,

Recognise the depths of our brokenness and the magnitude of our sinfulness that separated us from God. It is in this understanding that we find the urgency and necessity of Christ's redemptive work. Let His sacrifice serves as a constant reminder of His unconditional love and the restoration He offers to all who turn to Him. Embrace the truth that in Jesus, we find forgiveness, redemption, and eternal life, transforming our brokenness into wholeness and our despair into hope.

Exploring God's Redemptive Plan - Reflective Activity

Objective: This activity aims to encourage personal reflection on God's redemptive plan.

Instructions:

- Reflect on the question provided below.
- Write down your thoughts, feelings, and any insights that come to mind.
- Take your time and be honest with yourself as you engage in this reflective process.
- After completing the activity, consider discussing your response with a friend, mentor, or spiritual advisor for further insight and support.

Activity Question:

1. What do you perceive as the key elements or components of God's redemption plan, and how do they contribute to your faith journey?

_____
_____
_____

Reflection:
Consider any common themes, insights, or areas for further exploration. Think about God's redemptive plan in your life and how it continues to shape your understanding of His love, grace, and purpose for humanity. Consider how you can deepen your understanding of this plan and live in alignment with it.

THE DIVINE RESCUE:
Exploring God's Redemptive Plan

"Jesus is the one qualified mediator, the only qualified sacrifice, and the only qualified saviour." - Erwin W. Lutzer

Adam and Eve's disobedience marked the plunge of humanity into a state of total depravity, corrupting our entire being by the influence of sin. Yet, amidst this plight, God promised a pathway to redemption—a Saviour who would liberate humanity from sin's curse. This promise of redemption, beginning with the early proclamation in Genesis 3:15 and echoed through the prophetic verses in Isaiah 53, became a beacon of hope across generations.

In due time, God's redemptive design culminated in the incarnation of the eternal Logos. "In the beginning was the Word, and the Word was with God, and the Word was God. And the Word became flesh and dwelt among us, and we have seen His glory, glory as of the only Son from the Father, full of grace and truth" (John 1:1, 14). Through the incarnation, the Son of God emerged in human history as the embodiment of God's glory, grace, and truth, offering redemption from sin's grip through His sacrificial death and resurrection.

At the heart of God's redemptive plan stands the doctrine of election—God's sovereign and gracious choice of individuals before the world's inception (Ephesians 1:4–5). This doctrine doesn't diminish human responsibility but highlights the profound extent of God's grace to undeserving sinners.

Integral to God's plan is the call to repentance and faith. Repentance involves acknowledging our sinfulness and turning away from it, ushering sinners into the embrace of a merciful and loving God who welcomes those earnestly seeking Him. Saving faith, an assurance in Christ alone for salvation, is bestowed as a gift of grace, independent of human effort (Ephesians 2:8–9). Both repentance and faith are essential components for liberation from sin's bondage.

As the narrative of redemption unfolds, it unveils creation's ultimate purpose—complete restoration. It isn't merely a return to a pre-fall state but a cosmic rejuvenation where everything reconciles to God through Christ. This renewal encompasses the physical and spiritual realms, culminating in a new heavens and new earth (Colossians 1:19–20). The elect aren't only recipients of eternal salvation but also co-heirs and contributors to the restoration process. In the climax of redemptive history, God's love, sovereignty, and righteousness will shine brightly, and the redeemed, now perfected, will stand in His presence, experiencing complete joy.

God's redemption plan stands as a testament to His boundless love, mercy, and faithfulness towards humanity. From the beginning of time, He has been orchestrating a divine rescue mission to reconcile sinful humanity to Himself and restore the broken relationship caused by sin. Through the sacrificial death and resurrection of Christ, God provided the ultimate solution for sin, offering forgiveness, redemption, and eternal life to all who would believe in Him. This redemptive plan reveals the depth of God's compassion and the extent of His grace, inviting each of us to experience the fullness of His salvation and to walk in freedom and hope. As we embrace God's redemptive plan in our lives, may we be filled with gratitude and awe, forever transformed by His love and forever grateful for His saving grace.

Dear reader,

From the dawn of creation to the cross of Calvary, God's love and mercy have been at work, offering hope and salvation to all humanity. As we journey through life, let us marvel at the intricate details of His plan and trust in His sovereign purpose. May we find comfort in knowing that no matter our past mistakes or present struggles, God's redemptive power is always at work, offering forgiveness, restoration, and eternal life. Let us walk in faith, confident in His promises, and eager to share the Good News of His redeeming love with the world.

Reflecting on God's Redemptive Plan - Question Activity

Objective: This activity aims to stimulate personal reflection on the concept of God's redemptive plan.

Instructions:

- Reflect on the question provided below.
- Write down your thoughts, feelings, and any insights that arise.
- Take your time and be sincere in your responses.
- After completing the activity, consider discussing your insights with a friend or mentor for further exploration.

Activity Question:

1. How do you see God's redemptive plan unfolding in the world around you, and what role do you believe you play in it?

_____

_____

_____

Reflection:
Spend some time reviewing your response and contemplate its significance in your spiritual journey. Reflect on how your understanding of God's redemptive plan shapes your perspective and actions and consider how you can actively participate in His work of redemption in the world.

REDEEMING LOVE:
Unveiling the Mission of the Saviour

"Through the staggering goodness of Jesus Christ and His infinite Atonement, we can escape the deserved agonies of our moral failings and overcome the undeserved agonies of our mortal misfortunes."— Elder Matthew S. Holland

A redeemer is tasked with securing another's release from oppression, harm, or binding obligations. They restore lost freedoms by paying the required price, avenging wrongs, and setting the person free. In Christianity, the unique role of "Redeemer" belongs to Jesus Christ. He rescues believers from the dominion of darkness and leads them into the Kingdom of Light (Colossians 1:13–14).

In the Old Testament, the concept of redemption is conveyed through the verb "ga'al" which means "to buy back" or "to ransom." This term signifies God's act of redeeming Israel from slavery in Egypt (Exodus 6:6; 15:13). It unveils God's role as a deliverer, saving people from danger and captivity. Another term, "padah," symbolises redemption from sin through animal sacrifices (Psalm 26:11; 49:7; 103:8; Isaiah 1:27; 59:20). This points to God's redemptive plan to deliver us through Christ's sacrifice.

The New Testament develops the theme of redemption through the term "Lutron" which signifies "to redeem" or "to ransom," emphasising Christ's mission as the Redeemer who gave His life as a ransom for many (Matthew 20:28; Mark 10:45). His sacrificial death on the cross liberated sinners from the bondage of sin. Another New Testament term, "agorazein," highlights the costly nature of God's redemptive work in Christ (1 Corinthians 6:20; Galatians 4:5).

Christ, our Redeemer, paid the ultimate price for our freedom—His life. His sacrifice on the cross secured our liberation from sin and death, as testified in numerous scriptures (Acts 20:28; Ephesians 1:7; Hebrews 9:12–14; Revelation 1:5; 5:9–10). By His precious blood, we are redeemed from an empty life, forgiven, and cleansed from our sins.

Throughout the Bible, God's work of redemption points to Jesus as the supreme Redeemer of humanity (Isaiah 63:16). Christ embodies the fulfilment of the Scriptures' redemptive theme (Romans 3:25). Though our sins separated us from God, He sent His Son as our Redeemer to grant us eternal life (John 3:16; 10:10–11).

Believers are justified and saved from God's wrath through Christ (Romans 5:9). His sacrifice restores our fellowship with God, delivering us from evil forces and impending judgment. While our complete redemption awaits the future, we rejoice in the foretaste of this glory through the Holy Spirit within us.

In the eternal state, we shall fully experience the promised spiritual inheritance. Our Redeemer, Jesus, offers deliverance, freedom, and a profound future hope. As we await this glorious consummation, we celebrate the redemption and freedom He graciously grants us.

Dear reader,

The transformative power of God's redeeming love, a love that knows no bounds and reaches to the depths of our brokenness. Let His love be the anchor that steadies your soul in times of trial and uncertainty. As you reflect on His boundless grace and mercy, may it inspire you to extend that same love and compassion to others. Remember that in every circumstance, God's redeeming love offers hope, healing, and restoration. Let His love be the guiding light that illuminates your path and the source of strength that empowers you to live boldly for Him.

Unveiling the Mission of the Savior - Question Activity

Objective: This activity aims to stimulate personal reflection on the mission of Jesus Christ.

Instructions:

- Reflect on the question provided below.
- Write down your thoughts, feelings, and any insights that arise.
- Take your time and be sincere in your responses.
- After completing the activity, consider discussing your insights with a friend or mentor for further exploration.

Activity Question:

1. What do you believe was the primary mission of Jesus Christ during His time on Earth, and how does His mission impact your understanding of Him?

_____
_____
_____

Reflection:
Introspect on how the mission of Jesus Christ influences your beliefs, values, and relationship with Him, and consider how you can align your life with His mission.

THE COST OF GRACE:
Exploring the Price of Redemption

"The cost of redemption cannot be overstated. The wonders of grace cannot be overemphasised. Christ took the hell He didn't deserve so we could have the heaven we don't deserve."
- Randy Alcorn

At the cross, Jesus bore the punishment meant for our sins. Though innocent, He willingly endured death in our stead, a substitution where the righteous took the place of the unrighteous (1 Peter 3:18), the perfect offering for the corrupt. The doctrine of substitutionary atonement highlights that Christ suffered vicariously, substituting for the sinner and that His sufferings served to expiate the sins. Jesus took our place on the cross. He was made sin for us. He who knew no sin was made sin on our behalf, allowing us to become righteous through Him (2 Corinthians 5:21). Hanging on the cross, Christ bore the weight of the world's sins, carrying our guilt as the perfect Son of Man (1 Peter 2:24).

Jesus underwent physical death, not merely a natural passing but the death of a transgressor. Sin is the breach of God's law (1 John 3:4), and the soul that sins must face death (Ezekiel

18:4). While we all deserve death for our sins (Romans 3:23; 6:23), Christ's death pays our debt. Innocent of any crime (Luke 23:15), Jesus was executed as a criminal, His sinlessness making His death effective for us. Our legal debt stands paid in full— "tetelestai" (John 19:30). As the old gospel hymn echoes, "He paid a debt He did not owe; I owed a debt I could not pay."

Jesus also took our place judicially, bearing the penalty of sin and dying in our stead. "When you were dead in your sins . . ., God made you alive with Christ. He forgave us all our sins, having cancelled the charge of our legal indebtedness, which stood against us and condemned us; He has taken it away, nailing it to the cross" (Colossians 2:13–14). God erased all accusations against us on the cross. In Christ, believers are seen by God as guiltless since our offences have been punished in Jesus' body (Romans 8:1). Jesus' act of taking our place signifies God's immense love: "Greater love has no one than this: to lay down one's life for one's friends" (John 15:13). The penalty for sin extends beyond physical death to include a spiritual separation from God. In this aspect, too, Jesus took our place. A part of Christ's anguish on the cross was the feeling of forsakenness by the Father. After three hours of darkness, Jesus cried, "My God, my God, why have you forsaken me?" (Mark 15:34). Because of Christ's sacrifice, we need not experience that abandonment (Hebrews 13:5).

Jesus' suffering was intense. Before the crucifixion, He expressed distress (John 12:27). Those who tried to dissuade Him were rebuked—avoiding the ordeal was a temptation (Matthew 16:21–23), and Jesus had not come for an easy path. On the night of His arrest, Jesus was "overwhelmed with sorrow to the point of death" (Matthew 26:38). He even sweated blood (Luke 22:43–44). For our salvation, Jesus had to take our place and die for sin. He had to offer Himself as a sacrifice, for "without the shedding of blood, there is no forgiveness" (Hebrews 9:22). His sacrifice was perfect in holiness, worth, and power to save. After His resurrection, Jesus showed His scars to the apostles (John 20:26–27). These marks are an eternal reminder that He took our place, a testament to the eternalness of our Saviour's sacrifice (Revelation 5:6).

Dear reader,

As you reflect on the enormity of His sacrifice, may it ignite within you a deep sense of gratitude and awe. Let His sacrifice be a constant reminder of the lengths to which God is willing to go to redeem and restore us. May we never take lightly the price paid for our redemption, but instead, may it compel us to live lives worthy of His love and sacrifice, bringing glory to His name in all we do.

Exploring the Price of Redemption - Question Activity

Objective: This activity aims to prompt personal reflection on the cost of redemption.

Instructions:

- Reflect on the question provided below.
- Write down your thoughts, feelings, and any insights that arise.
- Take your time and be sincere in your responses.
- After completing the activity, consider discussing your insights with a friend or mentor for further exploration.

Activity Question:

1. What do you perceive as the price of redemption, and how does this understanding impact your appreciation for the sacrifice of Jesus Christ?

_____

_____

_____

Reflection:
Evaluate your response and consider its significance in your spiritual journey. Reflect on how your understanding of the price of redemption shapes your gratitude and devotion to Jesus Christ and consider how you can respond to His sacrifice in your daily life.

TURNING TOWARDS GRACE:
Understanding the Meaning of Repentance

"It is not the absence of sin but the grieving over it which distinguishes the child of God from empty professors" — A.W. Pink

The Tyndale Bible Dictionary defines power as the "ability to do things by virtue of strength, skill, resources, or authorisation." According to the Bible, a Christian's power comes from God through the Holy Spirit. The power of repentance grants freedom for usefulness and purpose. It grants access to power. A Christian's capability, that is his/her ability to accomplish anything significant is derived from the Holy Spirit. While many perceive repentance as "turning away from sin," remorse for sin and turning from it are linked to repentance but do not encapsulate its precise meaning. In the Bible, repent means "to change one's mind."

The Greek term for repentance is "Metanoia," signifying a shift in thinking. "Meta" means to change and "Noia" speaks to mind. Therefore, repent demands a reassessment of one's lifestyle that is to alter one's mindset, a transformation that occurs upon embracing God's perspective. What's intriguing is that as one draws closer to God, their sins become more apparent, leading to increased repentance. The more one comprehends God's goodness, the more apparent their own shortcomings.

The Bible emphasises that genuine repentance results in a change in behaviour. Therefore, repent—alter your inner self, your former way of thinking, regret past sins—and return to God—seek His purpose for your life—so that your sins may be wiped away, ushering in times of refreshing from the presence of the Lord. Repentance demands a complete turn towards God, necessitating a turn away from sin. Paul, in Acts 26:20, proclaims, "I preached that they should repent and turn to God and demonstrate their repentance by their deeds." As such, the Bible defines repentance as "a change of mind that leads to a change in action." Repentance and faith go hand in hand. Placing faith in Jesus Christ as the Saviour requires a prior shift in thinking about one's sin and recognising who Jesus is and what He has accomplished.

Repentance isn't an action to earn salvation. No one can repent and approach God unless drawn by Him. Instead, repentance is a gift from God, made possible only through His grace. The Bible underscores that genuine repentance leads to transformed actions. True repentance results in a change of conduct. This is why John the Baptist urged people to "produce fruit in keeping with repentance. "A sincere repentant heart demonstrates a changed life (Galatians 5:19–23). For instance, consider the story of Zacchaeus. He acknowledged, regretted, apologised for, and made amends for his past wrongdoings. Repentance signifies more than remorse; it signifies a commitment to change, to align one's life with principles of love, justice, and righteousness. Psalm 51:10 encapsulates this well: "Create in me a clean heart, O God, and renew a right spirit within me." Repentance embodies the redemptive power, inviting us to experience boundless mercy.

Repentance is the path to reconciliation, restoration, and transformation through God's grace. As seen in Luke 15:11-32, the parable of the prodigal son illustrates the joyous celebration that accompanies genuine repentance—a return to the loving embrace of our heavenly Father. Repentance isn't just for sinners; it's a call for all of us to acknowledge our errors, seek forgiveness, and commit to a better life. Ultimately, repentance is a transformative journey that demands examination of our hearts and a turning away from wrongdoing. It's an invitation to experience divine mercy and restore our relationship with God.

Dear reader,
Let grace be your compass, leading you towards a life of joy, peace, and purpose.

Understanding the Meaning of Repentance - Question Activity

Objective: This activity aims to prompt personal reflection on the concept of repentance.

Instructions:
- Reflect on the question provided below.
- Write down your thoughts, feelings, and any insights that arise.
- Take your time and be sincere in your responses.
- After completing the activity, consider discussing your insights with a friend or mentor for further exploration.

Activity Question:

1. What does repentance mean to you, and how do you perceive its significance in your spiritual journey?

_____

_____

_____

Reflection:
Consider your response and its significance in your spiritual growth. Reflect on how your understanding of repentance influences your relationship with God and shapes your actions and attitudes. Consider how you can deepen your practice of repentance and experience greater spiritual transformation.

THE FREEDOM OF FORGIVENESS:

Understanding the Essence of Forgiveness

"Forgiveness is not a feeling - it's a decision we make because we want to do what's right before God. It's a quality decision that won't be easy and it may take time to get through the process, depending on the severity of the offense." - Joyce Meyer

Forgiveness, as depicted in the Bible, signifies a "release" or a "dismissal" of something. In Christ, forgiveness involves releasing sinners from God's righteous penalty and entirely dismissing all charges against us (Romans 8:1). Colossians 1:14 highlights that in God's beloved Son, "we have redemption, the forgiveness of sins." The Amplified Bible renders the phrase as "the forgiveness of our sins [and the cancellation of sins' penalty]." Our gracious forgiveness from God for our sins serves as the gauge for how we extend forgiveness to others (Ephesians 4:32).

To some, forgiveness might seem synonymous with weakness or conceding victory to an undeserving individual, but it is unrelated to weakness or emotions. Instead, forgiveness is an act of the will. It's not given because someone deserves it—no one merits forgiveness. Forgiveness is a conscious display of love, mercy, and grace. It's a choice to release any grudge against another person, despite their actions toward you.

How does Forgiveness relate to Salvation?

Forgiveness is a fundamental aspect of salvation. When Jesus forgives us, our sins, trespasses, iniquities, and transgressions are wiped clean, completely erased from the record. Forgiveness of sin is akin to the erasure of a financial debt. When Jesus declared, "It is finished," from the cross (John 19:30), He essentially proclaimed, "It is paid in full" (tetelestai in Greek). Jesus bore the punishment we deserved, so when God forgives our sins, we're liberated; we no longer carry that debt. Our sins are wiped away, and God won't hold them against us (Psalm 103:12).

Salvation without forgiveness is impossible. Salvation is God's rescue from the consequences of sin. God's salvation in Christ epitomises extending forgiveness. Accepting God's forgiveness requires repentance and faith.

What about forgiving others?

Forgiveness is equally vital in the lives of believers. Ephesians 4:32 instructs, "Be kind and compassionate to one another, forgiving each other, just as in Christ God forgave you." Similarly, Colossians 3:13 advises, "Bear with each other and forgive whatever grievances you may have against one another. Forgive as the Lord forgave you." The crux in both passages is forgiving others as God has forgiven us. Why do we forgive? We do because we've been forgiven by the Lord. Forgiving others is demonstration of our love for God, our commitment to obedience and our will to empathy to another imperfect human being. The Bible emphasises forgiving those who wrong us. We don't keep a record of wrongs (1 Corinthians 13:5) but extend forgiveness as often as needed (Matthew 18:21–22). Refusing to forgive reveals resentment, bitterness, and anger—qualities unbefitting a maturing Christian. Biblically, forgiveness isn't solely offered by the offended person; it also requires the offender's acceptance, fostering reconciliation in relationships.

God promises that when we confess our sins and seek forgiveness, He freely grants it for Christ's sake (1 John 1:9). Similarly, the forgiveness we offer to others should have no bounds (Luke 17:3–4).

What are the benefits of forgiving others?

To further illustrate the benefits of forgiveness, I will share the story of a young woman named Maya, whose heart was burdened with the weight of bitterness and resentment. For years, Maya had harboured deep-seated anger towards her childhood friend, Sarah, who had betrayed her trust in a moment of weakness. Despite Sarah's apologies and attempts to reconcile, Maya stubbornly held onto her grudge, unwilling to forgive and move forward.

One day, as Maya sat alone in her room, wrestling with her feelings of resentment, she came across a passage in the Bible that spoke about the importance of forgiveness. Convicted by the words she read; Maya realised that her refusal to forgive was not only poisoning her own heart but also hindering her relationship with God.

Determined to break free from the chains of unforgiveness, Maya made a conscious decision to extend grace and forgiveness to Sarah. With trembling hands, she reached for her phone and dialled Sarah's number, her heart pounding with nervous anticipation.

When Sarah answered the call, Maya took a deep breath and uttered the words she had been longing to say for so long: "Sarah, I forgive you." Tears welled up in Maya's eyes as she felt the weight of bitterness lift from her soul, replaced by a sense of peace and liberation she had not known in years.

To her surprise, Sarah responded with tears of gratitude and relief, expressing how deeply sorry she was for the pain she had caused Maya. In that moment of vulnerability and reconciliation, Maya and Sarah's friendship was restored, stronger and more resilient than ever before.

As Maya hung up the phone, she felt a profound sense of joy and freedom wash over her. Through the act of forgiveness, she had not only healed her relationship with Sarah but had also experienced the transformative power of God's love and grace in her own life. From that day forward, Maya vowed to walk in forgiveness and extend grace to others, knowing that true healing and reconciliation could only be found through forgiveness.

Forgiving others brings numerous benefits that extend beyond the act itself. Firstly, forgiveness frees us from the burden of bitterness, resentment, and anger, allowing us to experience inner peace and emotional healing. By releasing the grip of unforgiveness, we open our hearts to love, joy, and positive relationships, both with others and with ourselves. Forgiveness also promotes reconciliation and restores broken relationships, fostering understanding, empathy, and unity. Moreover, forgiving others is an act of obedience to God's commandments, demonstrating our trust in His grace and mercy. Ultimately, the act of forgiveness not only benefits the recipient but also brings about transformation and renewal in the forgiver's life, paving the way for greater spiritual growth, healing, and freedom.

Dear reader,
Let forgiveness be the key that unlocks the door to reconciliation, restoration, and a life filled with joy and purpose.

Understanding the Essence of Forgiveness - Question Activity

Objective: This activity aims to prompt personal reflection on the concept of forgiveness.

Instructions:

- Reflect on the question provided below.
- Write down your thoughts, feelings, and any insights that arise.
- Take your time and be sincere in your responses.
- After completing the activity, consider discussing your insights with a friend or mentor for further exploration.

Activity Question:

1. What does forgiveness mean to you, and how do you believe it impacts your relationships, both with others and with God?

_____

_____

_____

Reflection:
Examine your response and consider its significance in your life. Reflect on how your understanding of forgiveness shapes your interactions with others and your spiritual journey. Consider how you can deepen your practice of forgiveness and experience greater emotional and spiritual freedom.

IMMERSED IN FAITH:
Understanding Water Baptism and Its Significance

"Baptism is not just about cleansing the body with water; it's about renewing the soul with faith."- Nicholas Robertson

Christian baptism, one of the ordinances instituted by Jesus for the church, was commanded by Him just before His ascension. He instructed His followers to make disciples of all nations, baptising them in the name of the Father, Son, and Holy Spirit, and teaching them to obey His commands (Matthew 28:19–20). This command underscores the church's responsibility to teach, disciple, and baptise believers until the end of time. Thus, baptism holds significance because it was commanded by Jesus Himself.

Although baptism predates the church's establishment, it was practiced in ancient times by Jews to symbolise the cleansed state of proselytes. John the Baptist also used baptism to prepare for the Lord's coming, emphasising repentance for all, not just Gentiles. However, John's baptism, representing repentance, differs from Christian baptism, as detailed in Acts 18:24–26 and 19:1–7. Christian baptism is distinct because it's done in the name of the Father, Son, and Holy Spirit. Through this act, a person is welcomed into the fellowship of the church. When saved, believers are spiritually baptised into the Body of Christ, symbolised by water baptism (1 Corinthians 12:13). Baptism publicly professes one's faith and discipleship. It silently declares, "I believe in Christ; He has cleansed my soul from sin, and I now live a sanctified life."

Christian baptism vividly illustrates Christ's death, burial, and resurrection, signifying our death to sin and new life in Him. As the believer confesses Jesus, they die to sin and rise to a renewed life (Romans 6:11, Colossians 2:12). Going into the water represents the burial of the old self, while emerging portrays the cleansed, holy life after salvation (Romans 6:4). Baptism is an outward declaration of the inner transformation in a believer's life. Though closely linked to salvation, it's not a prerequisite for it. The Bible consistently presents the sequence of belief followed by baptism (Acts 2:41, Acts 16:14–15).

New believers should seek baptism promptly, as seen in the Ethiopian eunuch's immediate desire to be baptised after hearing Philip's message about Jesus (Acts 8:35–36). Baptism is a profound symbol of a believer's identification with Christ's death, burial, and resurrection, to be observed wherever the gospel is preached and embraced.

Understanding Water Baptism and Its Significance - Question Activity

Objective: This activity aims to prompt personal reflection on the practice of water baptism and its significance.

Instructions:

- Reflect on the question provided below.
- Write down your thoughts, feelings, and any insights that arise.
- Take your time and be sincere in your responses.
- After completing the activity, consider discussing your insights with a friend or mentor for further exploration.

Activity Question:

1. What is your understanding of water baptism, and why do you believe it holds significance in the Christian faith?

_____

_____

_____

Reflection:
Consider how you can deepen your understanding of this sacrament and its importance in your walk with God.

SUBMERGED IN GRACE:
Examining the Purpose of Baptism

"Baptism is the outward expression of an inward transformation, a symbol of our commitment to walk in the newness of life found in Christ."- Nicholas Robertson

Believers in Christ are encouraged to undergo baptism, an act reflective of their obedience to Jesus' teachings. In the Great Commission, Christ urged His disciples to baptise all nations, emphasising the importance of this ritual as part of discipleship (Matthew 28:18–20). Being baptised, therefore, aligns with the essence of being a devoted follower of Christ.

Baptism isn't a means of salvation but symbolises an inner transformation. It visually represents the cleansing from sin, echoing Christ's death, burial, and resurrection on behalf of the believer. It serves as a visible sign of the believer's unity with Christ.

Historically, baptism held significance in first-century Judaism, initially reserved for Gentile converts. However, when John baptised Jews, it signified a collective acknowledgment of sinfulness and the need for repentance.

The act of baptism was a public declaration of one's repentance in anticipation of Christ's coming.

In the early church, baptism became a defining marker of genuine faith. Those not baptised weren't typically recognised as part of the Christian community. It was a decisive step, often leading to social ostracisation, particularly for Jewish converts facing separation from family and synagogue.

Though baptism doesn't inherently grant salvation, it openly declares one's commitment to Christ and, in many cultures, exposes individuals to potential persecution. As an act of obedience to Christ, believers are encouraged to partake in baptism, symbolising the cleansing of sins, spiritual rebirth, and public proclamation of their Christian identity.

Dear reader,
As you are submerged in grace, let go of guilt, shame, and self-condemnation, knowing that you are unconditionally loved and accepted by your Heavenly Father. Allow His grace to wash over you, cleansing you of past mistakes and empowering you to live boldly in His love. Embrace the freedom and renewal that come from being submerged in grace, and let it overflow into every aspect of your life, radiating hope and compassion to all you encounter.

Examining the Purpose of Baptism - Question Activity

Objective: This activity aims to prompt personal reflection on the purpose of baptism.

Instructions:

- Reflect on the question provided below.
- Write down your thoughts, feelings, and any insights that arise.
- Take your time and be sincere in your responses.
- After completing the activity, consider discussing your insights with a friend or mentor for further exploration.

Activity Question:

1. What do you believe is the purpose of baptism, and how does this practice align with your understanding of faith and discipleship?

_____

_____

_____

Reflection:
How has your understanding of baptism shaped your beliefs and practices as a follower of Christ.

HOLINESS IN ACTION:
Exploring the Meaning of Sanctification

"Sanctification is the ongoing journey of becoming more like Christ, a process of God's grace working within us to transform our hearts and minds."- Unknown.

Sanctification, rooted in the word "saint," signifies holiness. It involves setting apart something for special use or making a person holy. Jesus addressed this in John 17, highlighting that believers are distinct from the world and praying for their sanctification through truth—God's Word (John 17:16-17). In Christian theology, sanctification begins at rebirth, marking believers as separated unto God (1 Corinthians 1:30; Hebrews 10:10), often termed as "positional" sanctification, closely linked to justification.

While believers are positionally holy, set free from sin's bondage by Christ's sacrifice (Acts 13:39), they still grapple with sin (1 John 1:10). This practical aspect is known as "progressive" or "experiential" sanctification, where obedience to God's Word shapes spiritual growth and maturity (2 Peter 3:18). It's a lifelong journey, initiated and continued by God (Philippians 1:6), pursued ardently by believers (1 Peter 1:15; Hebrews 12:14), and influenced by the application of Scripture (John 17:17).

Progressive sanctification aligns believers with their mission in the world, mirroring Christ's sanctified purpose (John 17:18–19). As Jesus set Himself apart for God's plan, believers are similarly set apart for His purpose (John 10:36). This process mirrors our Lord's sanctification, making us "saints" or "sanctified ones." Previously, our conduct marked our separation from God; now it reflects our standing before Him, gradually aligning us with Christ's likeness daily (Hebrews 10:14).

Scripture presents a "complete" or "ultimate" sanctification akin to glorification, foreseen in 1 Thessalonians 5:23 and linked to Christ's return (Colossians 1:27; Colossians 3:4). This ultimate sanctification will eradicate sin entirely, ushering believers into total separation from sin's presence— a state of complete holiness or glorification (1 John 3:2). Sanctification includes past justification—granting positional holiness, present progressive growth towards maturity, and future glorification—an ultimate and permanent separation from sin in all aspects. These phases of sanctification free believers from sin's penalty, empower them over sin, and promise complete liberation from sin's presence.

Dear reader,

Let holiness be your hallmark, shining brightly as a beacon of light in a world longing for truth and authenticity.

Exploring the Meaning of Sanctification - Question Activity

Objective: This activity aims to prompt personal reflection on the concept of sanctification.

Instructions:

- Reflect on the question provided below.
- Write down your thoughts, feelings, and any insights that arise.
- Take your time and be sincere in your responses.
- After completing the activity, consider discussing your insights with a friend or mentor for further exploration.

Activity Question:

1. What does sanctification mean to you, and how do you perceive its importance in the Christian journey of spiritual growth?

_____

_____

_____

Reflection:
Reflect on how your understanding of sanctification shapes your beliefs and practices as a follower of Christ.

CHOSEN AS HEIRS:
Exploring the Meaning of Adoption in Christ

"Adoption in Christ is not merely a legal transaction; it is a divine declaration of belonging, a sacred invitation into the family of God's boundless love."- Nicholas Robertson

Adoption is the legal act of making someone a son or daughter. It's a metaphor in the Bible that explains how Christians enter God's family. Jesus came to enable this adoption: "He adopted you as His own children" (Romans 8:15, NLT) and "that we might receive adoption to sonship" (Galatians 4:5).

The Bible uses both the metaphors of being "born again" (John 3:3) and "adopted" to describe how individuals become part of God's family. Although these metaphors seem contradictory—since birth and adoption are typically exclusive concepts—they should be seen as figurative and complementary, not conflicting.

Adoption wasn't prevalent in Jewish society where status was based on birth. In contrast, the Roman world widely practiced adoption. In Roman times, a man primarily passed his wealth to his sons. If there were no sons or if they were unsuitable heirs, adoption was the recourse. Unlike modern infant adoptions, older boys or adult men were usually adopted. Upon legal approval, the adoptee's debts were forgiven, and a new name was given. This person became the legal son of the adoptive father, entitled to all rights and benefits of a son. While a father could disown his natural-born son, an adoption was irrevocable.

Paul used the metaphor of adoption in his writings to Roman audiences who understood it. He likened Christians' adoption by God to Roman adoption practices. Galatians 4:3–7 illustrates this: God sent His Son to redeem them, granting them adoption. Christians, formerly enslaved, are now heirs as God's adopted children. Upon faith in Christ, Christians experience the cancellation of debts, are bestowed with a new name, and receive the full rights of God's heirs. However, unlike Roman adoption where worthiness mattered, God adopts individuals purely out of His grace, irrespective of their worthiness.

Thus, Christians are metaphorically both born into and adopted into God's family, culminating in a permanent place within His family. Both metaphors reveal the incredible truth that believers belong to God's eternal family.

Christ stands as a proof of the depth of God's love and the richness of His grace. Through the sacrifice of Jesus Christ, we have been chosen and embraced as beloved children of God, heirs to His kingdom and recipients of His unfailing love. As we walk in the reality of our adoption, we must be filled with gratitude and awe, forever transformed by the truth of our identity in Christ. We must embrace our role as heirs of God's promises, living each day with confidence, purpose, and the assurance of His unending love and care.

Dear reader,
Let the reality of your identity as a beloved child of God sink deep into your heart. As heirs, we inherit the blessings and promises of God's kingdom, including His unconditional love, forgiveness, and eternal life. Let this truth anchor your soul and fuel your sense of purpose and belonging. As you walk in the confidence of your adoption, may you live boldly as a representative of God's grace and love to the world. Celebrate the privilege of being chosen and embrace the responsibility to live as a cherished member of God's family.

Exploring the Meaning of Adoption in Christ - Question Activity

Objective: This activity aims to prompt personal reflection on the concept of adoption in Christ.

Instructions:

- Reflect on the question provided below.
- Write down your thoughts, feelings, and any insights that arise.
- Take your time and be sincere in your responses.
- After completing the activity, consider discussing your insights with a friend or mentor for further exploration.

Activity Question:

1. What does adoption in Christ mean to you, and how does this concept impact your identity and relationship with God?

_____

_____

_____

Reflection:
Reflect on how your understanding of adoption in Christ shapes your beliefs and practices as a follower of Christ.

FROM DARKNESS TO LIGHT:
Unveiling the Power of Regeneration

"Regeneration is not a mere renovation; it's a radical rebirth, a transformative work of God's Spirit within us, breathing new life into our weary souls."- Nicholas Robertson

Regeneration, also known as rebirth, is intricately tied to the concept of being "born again," a term often linked to spiritual renewal in the Bible. It stands distinct from our initial physical birth where we inherit a sinful nature. This rebirth is a spiritual transformation, breathing new life into us spiritually. Before this renewal, we are spiritually lifeless and mired in transgressions until Christ brings about this regeneration through faith (Ephesians 2:1).

This process of regeneration is radical. Just as our physical birth introduces us into the earthly realm, our spiritual rebirth ushers us into the heavenly sphere (Ephesians 2:6). Post-regeneration, our perceptions change, inclining us toward divine matters; we begin to live lives characterised by faith and righteousness. Christ is now formed within us; we partake in a divine nature, having become new creations (2 Corinthians 5:17). This transformation originates from God; it is His power, grace, and mercy that bring about this rebirth (Ephesians 2:1, 8). The same divine power that resurrected

Christ from the dead is at work in the regeneration and conversion of sinners (Ephesians 1:19–20).

Regeneration is not optional but necessary. Our sinful nature is incompatible with God's presence. Jesus emphasised to Nicodemus the need for spiritual rebirth to perceive the kingdom of God (John 3:3, 7). Regeneration is essential; while physical birth suits us for life on earth, spiritual rebirth equips us for heavenly existence. Scripture affirms this necessity in passages like Ephesians 2:1; 1 Peter 1:23; John 1:13; 1 John 3:9; 4:7; 5:1, 4, 18. Regeneration is a crucial aspect of God's work at the moment of salvation alongside sealing (Ephesians 1:14), adoption (Galatians 4:5), reconciliation (2 Corinthians 5:18–20), among others. It's God's act of making a person spiritually alive through faith in Jesus Christ. Before salvation, we weren't God's children (John 1:12–13); instead, we were under wrath (Ephesians 2:3; Romans 5:18–20). Pre-salvation, we were degenerate; post-salvation, we're regenerated. The outcome of this rebirth is peace with God (Romans 5:1), new life (Titus 3:5; 2 Corinthians 5:17), and eternal sonship (John 1:12–13; Galatians 3:26). Regeneration initiates the process of sanctification, shaping us into God's intended people (Romans 8:28–30).

The sole pathway to regeneration is through faith in Christ's accomplished work on the cross. No volume of good deeds or adherence to the Law can regenerate the heart. "No human being will be justified in [God's] sight by works of the law" (Romans 3:20). Only Christ offers a remedy for the inherent depravity of the human heart. We don't need renovation or reform; what's needed is rebirth.

Dear reader,
Let go of the old and welcome the new, as His Spirit works within you to renew and restore. As you experience the power of regeneration, allow it to reshape your thoughts, desires, and actions, aligning them with His perfect will. Embrace the freedom and possibility that come from being made new in Christ and let His love and grace flow through you to touch the lives of others. May the power of regeneration be a constant reminder of God's faithfulness and the endless possibilities found in Him.

Unveiling the Power of Regeneration - Question Activity

Objective: This activity aims to prompt personal reflection on the power of regeneration in the Christian faith.

Instructions:

- Reflect on the question provided below.
- Write down your thoughts, feelings, and any insights that arise.
- Take your time and be sincere in your responses.
- After completing the activity, consider discussing your insights with a friend or mentor for further exploration.

Activity Question:

1. What does the power of regeneration mean to you, and how have you experienced its transformative impact in your life?

_____

_____

_____

Reflection:
Consider how you can continue to embrace and cooperate with God's regenerative work in your life for ongoing spiritual growth and renewal.

CLOTHED IN ETERNAL SPLENDOUR:
Exploring the Meaning of Glorification

"Glorification is the culmination of our journey of faith, the moment when our earthly limitations are transformed into heavenly splendour, and we stand in the presence of God, radiating His glory for eternity."- Nicholas Robertson

Glorification is the final stage of the believer's journey of faith, marking the culmination of God's redemptive plan. It is the moment when those who have been redeemed by the blood of Jesus Christ are transformed into their glorified state, free from the effects of sin and fully conformed to the image of Christ. Glorification entails the resurrection of the body to eternal life, where believers will experience the fullness of God's presence and enjoy unending fellowship with Him. It is a moment of surpassing joy and eternal bliss, where every tear will be wiped away, and every pain and sorrow will be no more. Glorification is the ultimate fulfilment of God's promise to His children, as they are welcomed into His eternal kingdom to reign with Him forever.

Glorification shows God's ultimate eradication of sin from the lives of the saints—those who are saved—during the eternal state (Romans 8:18; 2 Corinthians 4:17). At Christ's advent, God's glory—His honour, praise, majesty, and holiness—will be fully realised in us. We'll cease to be mortals weighed down by sin; instead, we'll undergo a transformative change into holy immortals, directly accessing God's presence unhindered and relishing holy communion with Him for all eternity. When considering glorification, our focus should be on Christ, the "blessed hope" of every Christian, and view final glorification as the pinnacle of sanctification.

The ultimate glorification awaits the revelation of the glory of our great God and Saviour Jesus Christ (Titus 2:13; 1 Timothy 6:14). Until His return, we grapple with sin, and our spiritual vision remains distorted due to the curse. "For now, we see in a mirror dimly, but then face to face. Now I know in part; then I shall know fully, even as I have been fully known" (1 Corinthians 13:12). Daily, empowered by the Spirit, we strive to put to death the "fleshly" (sinful) aspects within us (Romans 8:13).

How and when does final glorification occur?

At the sound of the last trumpet and Christ's arrival, believers will undergo an instantaneous, fundamental transformation ("we shall all be changed, in a moment, in the twinkling of an eye" – 1 Corinthians 15:51). Then, the "perishable" will be clothed with the "imperishable" (1 Corinthians 15:53). Yet, 2 Corinthians 3:18 reveals a mysterious ongoing transformation in the present: believers "with unveiled face" behold the glory of the Lord and are being transformed into His image "from one degree of glory to another" (2 Corinthians 3:18). This transformation, part of sanctification, is not exclusive to particularly saintly individuals; it's a blessing bestowed upon every believer. This doesn't refer to our final glorification but signifies an aspect of sanctification wherein the Spirit is continually transfiguring us. All praise to Him for sanctifying us in the Spirit and truth (Jude 24-25; John 17:17; 4:23).

Understanding Scripture's teachings on the nature of glory—both God's unmatched glory and our participation in it at His return—is crucial. God's glory encompasses not only the unapproachable light He dwells in (1 Timothy 6:15-16) but also His honour (Luke 2:13) and holiness. Psalm 104:2 refers to the same God mentioned in 1 Timothy 6:15-16; He is "clothed with splendour and majesty," enveloping Himself "with light as with a garment" (Psalm 104:2; cf. 93:1; Job 37:22; 40:10). When the Lord Jesus returns in His great glory to execute judgment (Matthew 24:29-31; 25:31-35), He'll do so as the only Sovereign with eternal dominion (1 Timothy 6:14-16).

Created beings dare not gaze upon God's awesome glory; like Ezekiel (Ezekiel 1:4-29) and Simon Peter (Luke 5:8), Isaiah was overwhelmed by self-loathing in the presence of the all-holy God. After the seraphim proclaimed, "Holy, holy, holy is the Lord of hosts; the whole earth is full of his glory!" Isaiah exclaimed, "Woe is me! For I am lost; for I am a man of unclean lips, and I dwell in the midst of a people of unclean lips; for my eyes have seen the King, the Lord of hosts!" (Isaiah 6:4). Even the seraphim demonstrated unworthiness to gaze upon divine glory, covering their faces with their wings.

God's glory may be considered "weighty" or "heavy"; the Hebrew word "kabod" literally means "heavy or burdensome." Scripturally, "kabod" is often figurative, portraying the "weightiness" of a person who is honourable, impressive, or deserving of respect. When the Lord Jesus became incarnate, He revealed both the "weighty" holiness of God and the fullness of His grace and truth ("and the Word became flesh and dwelt among us, and we have seen his glory, glory as of the only Son from the Father, full of grace and truth" [John 1:14; cf. 17:1–5]). The glory revealed by the incarnate Christ accompanies the ministry of the Spirit (2 Corinthians 3:7); it is unchanging and permanent (Isaiah 4:6-7; cf. Job 14:2; Psalm 102:11; 103:15; James 1:10). Previous manifestations of God's glory were transient, like the fading radiance from Moses' face. Moses veiled his face to conceal the waning glory from the hard-hearted Israelites (1 Corinthians 3:12), yet through Christ, the veil has been lifted, and we reflect the glory of the Lord, striving by the Spirit to emulate Him.

In His high priestly prayer, the Lord Jesus asked God to sanctify us by His truth (i.e., make us holy; John 17:17); sanctification is essential to behold Jesus' glory and share eternal fellowship with Him (John 17:21-24). "Father, I desire that they also, whom you have given me, may be with me where I am, to see my glory that you have given me because you loved me before the foundation of the world" (John 17:24). If the glorification of the saints aligns with the pattern revealed in Scripture, it must involve our participation in the glory (i.e., holiness) of God. According to Philippians 3:20–21, our citizenship is in heaven, and when our Saviour returns, He'll transform our humble bodies "to be like His glorious body." While it hasn't been fully revealed what we shall become, we know that, at His return in great glory, we'll be like Him, for we'll see Him as He is (1 John 3:2). We'll perfectly conform to the image of our Lord Jesus, liberated from sin and its consequences. Our blessed hope should inspire us towards holiness, aided by the Spirit. "Everyone who thus hopes in Him purifies himself as He is pure" (1 John 3:3).

Exploring the Meaning of Glorification - Question Activity

Objective: This activity aims to prompt personal reflection on the concept of glorification in the Christian faith.

Instructions:

- Reflect on the question provided below.
- Write down your thoughts, feelings, and any insights that arise.
- Take your time and be sincere in your responses.
- After completing the activity, consider discussing your insights with a friend or mentor for further exploration.

Activity Question:

1. What does glorification mean to you as a Christian, and how does this concept shape your understanding of eternity and the fulfilment of God's promises?

_____

_____

_____

Reflection:
Consider how you can live in anticipation of the ultimate glorification that awaits believers and how it motivates you to live a life that honours and glorifies God.

FOLLOWING IN HIS FOOTSTEPS:
Understanding the Identity of a Disciple

"A disciple is not just a follower, but a devoted learner, imitator, and ambassador of the teachings and example of their Master."

The core of being a disciple resides in the deep commitment to follow, embrace, and actively share the teachings of another. In the Christian context, a disciple is someone who walks in the footsteps of Jesus Christ, passionately embraces, and disseminates the profound tidings of salvation through Him. Christian discipleship is the transformative journey through which adherents grow in their relationship with Jesus Christ and are empowered by the Holy Spirit to navigate life's tribulations, gradually resembling Christ more and more. This transformative expedition demands believers to heed the Holy Spirit's beckoning, scrutinising their thoughts, words, and actions in alignment with the Scriptures. Immersion in the Word becomes a daily necessity—studying, praying, and aligning with its teachings. Simultaneously, readiness to articulate the reason behind the hope within us (1 Peter 3:15) and to mentor others on the path of Christlikeness becomes paramount.

According to the Scriptures, Christian discipleship unfurls as a personal evolution, marked by the following attributes:

- **Placing Jesus Above All (Mark 8:34–38):** A true disciple must be distinct from the world, centre their focus on Christ, and endeavour to honour Him in every facet of existence. Shedding self-absorption for Christ-centred living becomes a foundational pursuit. Adherence to Jesus' Teachings is paramount (John 8:31–32). Obedience is the litmus test of faith. Following Christ's teachings and being doers of the Word becomes pivotal (James 1:22). Jesus Himself epitomised obedience, exemplifying complete submission to the Father, even unto death (Philippians 2:6–8). Bearing Fruit (John 15:5–8): Christian disciples are meant to live purposefully, yielding the fruit of the Spirit, displaying good works and righteousness (Hebrews 12:11). While fruit production isn't our direct mandate, abiding in Christ bears this fruit, fulfilling God's desire for an abundant harvest (John 15:1–8).

- **Demonstrating Love for Fellow Disciples (John 13:34–35):** Genuine affection for other believers is evidence of our kinship in God's family (1 John 3:10). Love, as detailed in 1 Corinthians 13, is portrayed as an action rather than mere emotion. Esteeming others, selflessly considering their interests, and exhibiting patience are manifestations of true love (Philippians 2:3–4; 1 Peter 4:8).

- **Multiplying Disciples (Matthew 28:18–20):** Discipleship is a continuum. Christ's parting directive to His followers was to "make disciples of all nations" (Matthew 28:19). This necessitates both evangelism—sharing the Gospel and urging repentance—and active mentorship. Christians are called to engage in training individuals, perpetuating a cycle where trained individuals become mentors themselves, perpetuating the pattern modelled by Christ (2 Timothy 2:2).

A Christian disciple epitomises one who prioritises Christ, follows His commands, yields good fruit, exhibits love, and actively engages in disciple-making. Such an individual becomes a powerful agent, impacting the world for the glory of God in this fallen realm.

Dear reader,
Let your identity as a disciple fuel your passion for His kingdom, as you strive to live out His teachings and bring glory to His name. May you find strength and purpose in the identity of a disciple, and may your life be a testimony to His grace and goodness.

Understanding the Identity of a Disciple - Question Activity

Objective: This activity aims to prompt personal reflection on the identity of a disciple.

Instructions:

- Reflect on the question provided below.
- Write down your thoughts, feelings, and any insights that arise.
- Take your time and be sincere in your responses.
- After completing the activity, consider discussing your insights with a friend or mentor for further exploration.

Activity Question:

1. What does it mean to you to be a disciple of Jesus Christ, and how does this identity influence your beliefs, values, and actions?

_____

_____

_____

Reflection:
Reflect on how your identity as a disciple shapes your relationship with Jesus, your commitment to following Him, and your role in His kingdom purposes.

LIVING IN RIGHTEOUSNESS:
Understanding the Concept of Moral Excellence

"Righteousness is not just about obeying rules; it's about aligning our hearts with God's will and living in harmony with His truth and love."- Nicholas Robertson

The concept of righteousness, as defined by dictionaries, denotes behaviour that aligns with accepted moral and just standards. In the Bible, righteousness mirrors God's perfection across every attribute, attitude, behaviour, and word. God's laws, outlined in the Bible, not only reflect His character but also serve as the benchmark against which human righteousness is measured. In the Greek New Testament, "righteousness" predominantly refers to conduct concerning others, encompassing the rights of individuals in various spheres like business, legal affairs, and particularly in relation to God. It stands in contrast to wickedness, the behaviour arising from self-centredness that lacks reverence for God and respect for others. The righteous, as described in the Bible, are just and upright, adhering to God and placing trust in Him (Psalm 33:18–22). The challenging reality is that achieving true and flawless righteousness independently is beyond human capability due to the lofty standard it requires. However, the good news is that genuine righteousness becomes attainable for humanity through Jesus Christ's cleansing of sin and the presence of the Holy Spirit within. Our own efforts cannot secure righteousness, yet Christians are endowed with the righteousness of Christ. "God made Him who had no sin to be sin for us so that in Him we might become the righteousness of God" (2 Corinthians 5:21). This truth is astounding at the cross, Jesus swapped our sin for His faultless righteousness, allowing us to stand before God, not cloaked in our sin, but adorned in the pure righteousness of Jesus. This means that, in the eyes of God, we are deemed righteous—accepted and treated as such—because of what the Lord Jesus accomplished. He bore our sin, and in turn, we receive His righteousness. On the cross, Jesus bore the treatment for sins He never committed, while we are treated as righteous despite our flaws. Through Christ's sacrificial endurance, we're regarded as fulfilling God's Law completely, absolved from its penalty. This gift of righteousness is bestowed upon us by the merciful and gracious God.

Dear reader,
Let integrity, virtue, and righteousness be the guiding principles of your life, shaping your character and actions.

Understanding the Concept of Moral Excellence - Question Activity

Objective: This activity aims to prompt personal reflection on the concept of moral excellence.

Instructions:
- Reflect on the question provided below.
- Write down your thoughts, feelings, and any insights that arise.
- Take your time and be sincere in your responses.
- After completing the activity, consider discussing your insights with a friend or mentor for further exploration.

Activity Question:

1. What does moral excellence mean to you, and how do you believe it shapes one's character and behaviour?

_____

_____

_____

Reflection:
Consider how you can cultivate moral excellence in your life and contribute positively to your community and society.

THE CALL TO PURITY:
Understanding the Concept of Holiness

"Holiness is not a list of rules to follow; it's a lifestyle of surrender to God's will, a journey of becoming more like Him in every aspect of our lives."- Nicholas Robertson

Holiness epitomises the very nature of God, embodying His absolute purity, righteousness, and flawlessness. It calls believers to separate themselves from worldly influences and adhere to God's standards of moral excellence. Holiness necessitates dedicating every facet of our lives to God, relinquishing our own desires and ambitions to align with His divine will. It constitutes a journey of inner transformation, allowing the Holy Spirit to mould our thoughts, words, and deeds to mirror the character of Christ. Rather than striving for flawlessness, holiness entails a continual process of growth and sanctification, drawing nearer to God and resembling Him more with each passing day.

In 1 Peter 1:13-16, Peter urges believers to prepare their minds for action, to maintain a clear and sober spirit, and to anchor their hope on the grace they will receive when Jesus

Christ is revealed. He instructs them as obedient children not to conform to their former desires from the time of ignorance. Instead, they are called to emulate the Holy One who summoned them, to demonstrate holiness in every aspect of their conduct, referencing Leviticus 11:44 and Leviticus 19:2.

Understanding God's holiness is crucial. 1 Samuel 2:2 and Isaiah 6:3 underscore God's unmatched perfection. His holiness denotes absolute flawlessness, setting Him apart (Hosea 11:9). His essence is utterly devoid of any trace of sin (James 1:13; Hebrews 6:18). He stands far above all, incomparable to any other (Psalm 40:5). This holiness defines every aspect of His character—His love, mercy, anger, and wrath—all are characterised by His divine holiness, a concept challenging for human understanding.

What then does holiness mean for us?

In Leviticus, God directed Israel to distinct living—separate from other nations—by providing specific guidelines. Chosen by God, Israel was set apart, given standards to showcase their belonging to Him. Similarly, Peter addresses believers in 1 Peter 1:16, emphasising the call to live "set apart" from the world, following God's standards, not the world. This call isn't about achieving perfection but about standing out from the world. Believers, described as "a holy nation" in 1 Peter 2:9, are set apart; it's a reality to be lived out daily, as Peter guides in 1 Peter 1:13-16.

How do we attain holiness?
Holiness stems solely from a right relationship with God through faith in Jesus Christ as Saviour, accepting His gift of eternal life. Pursuing holiness without this foundation is futile. Therefore, ensuring our belief in Christ for salvation is paramount (John 3). For believers, our position in Christ already distinguishes us (1 Peter 2:9). As we maintain daily living set apart from the world, our pursuit involves aligning with God's Word, studying it, and growing in its principles.

Dear reader,
The pursuit of holiness is central to the Christian faith, as believers are called to reflect the character of God and strive for moral excellence in all aspects of their lives. Holiness involves a continual process of sanctification, whereby individuals are transformed by the Holy Spirit to become more like Christ. It is not merely an external conformity to religious rituals or rules but a genuine inward transformation of the heart, mind, and soul. Ultimately, holiness is both a gift of God's grace and a lifelong journey of growth and spiritual maturity, leading to a deeper intimacy with God and a life that honours and glorifies Him in all things.

Understanding the Concept of Holiness - Question Activity

Objective: This activity aims to prompt personal reflection on the concept of holiness.

Instructions:

- Reflect on the question provided below.
- Write down your thoughts, feelings, and any insights that arise.
- Take your time and be sincere in your responses.
- After completing the activity, consider discussing your insights with a friend or mentor for further exploration.

Activity Question:

1. What does holiness mean to you, and how do you perceive its importance in the Christian faith and in your personal life?

_____

_____

_____

Reflection:
Consider how you can pursue holiness in your daily life and strive to reflect the character of God in all you do.

INFINITE MAJESTY:
Discovering the Identity of God

"God is the beginning and the end, the creator of all things, and the source of unending love and boundless grace."- Nicholas Robertson

To fathom the entirety of God's nature is an insurmountable feat for any human mind. Job's companion's words echo this sentiment: "Can you find out the deep things of God? Can you find out the limit of the Almighty? It is higher than heaven—what can you do? Deeper than Sheol—what can you know?" (Job 11:7-8). Isaiah 55:9 portrays God's voice: "For as the heavens are higher than the earth, so are my ways higher than your ways and my thoughts than your thoughts." Despite this, God has, through the Bible and other means, unveiled elements of His being.

Though our understanding remains veiled, we are beckoned to earnestly seek the Lord (1 Corinthians 13:12; Hebrews 11:6).

Who is God?

God is the creator and sustainer of the universe, the supreme being who exists outside of time and space. He is infinite in power, knowledge, and presence, transcending human comprehension. God is characterised by His attributes of love, mercy, justice, and holiness. He is the source of all life and the ultimate authority over all creation. Across various religious traditions, God is understood in different ways, but in Christianity, God is revealed as a triune being—Father, Son, and Holy Spirit. This belief underscores the relational nature of God, who desires a personal and intimate relationship with humanity. Through His divine revelation in Scripture and through the life, death, and resurrection of Jesus Christ, God invites humanity into a journey of faith, redemption, and eternal fellowship with Him. Let us explore what Scripture reveals about God:

The Unquestionable Reality: The existence of God is so apparent, resonating through creation and human conscience, that the Bible deems an atheist a "fool" (Psalm 14:1). The Bible doesn't aim to prove God's existence; it assumes it from the outset (Genesis 1:1). It illuminates God's nature, character, and actions.

The Defining Essence: Accurate perception of God holds paramount importance, for a misconstrued notion leads to idolatry. Psalm 50:21 finds God reproaching the wicked: "You thought I was altogether like you." Initially, a concise definition of God encapsulates "the Supreme Being; the Creator and Ruler of all that is; the Self-existent One, perfect in power, goodness, and wisdom."

His Attributes: We comprehend certain truths about God because, in His mercy, He has disclosed some of His qualities. God is spirit, intangible by nature (John 4:24). He is One, yet exists as three Persons—God the Father, God the Son, and God the Holy Spirit (Matthew 3:16-17). God is infinite (1 Timothy 1:17), incomparable (2 Samuel 7:22), and immutable (Malachi 3:6). God is omnipresent (Psalm 139:7-12), omniscient (Psalm 147:5; Isaiah 40:28), and omnipotent (Ephesians 1; Revelation 19:6).

His Attributes: God's character is unveiled in the Bible: just (Acts 17:31), loving (Ephesians 2:4-5), truthful (John 14:6), and holy (1 John 1:5). God exhibits compassion (2 Corinthians 1:3), mercy (Romans 9:15), and grace (Romans 5:17). God judges sin (Psalm 5:5) yet extends forgiveness (Psalm 130:4).

His Actions: Understanding God is intertwined with His deeds, as His actions emanate from His essence. Here's a condensed list of God's works—past, present, and future: creation (Genesis 1:1; Isaiah 42:5); sustenance of creation (Colossians 1:17); execution of His eternal plan (Ephesians 1:11) involving human redemption from sin's curse and death (Galatians 3:13-14); drawing people to Christ (John 6:44); disciplining His children (Hebrews 12:6); and final judgment (Revelation 20:11-15).

The Path to Relationship: In the form of the Son, God incarnated (John 1:14). The Son of God became the Son of Man, bridging the gap between God and humanity (John 14:6; 1 Timothy 2:5). Solely through the Son, we obtain forgiveness (Ephesians 1:7), reconciliation with God (John 15:15; Romans 5:10), and eternal salvation (2 Timothy 2:10). In Jesus Christ "all the fullness of the Deity lives in bodily form" (Colossians 2:9). To truly comprehend God, we simply gaze upon Jesus.

The Bible acknowledges God as the Creator of all: "In the beginning, God created the heavens and the earth" (Genesis 1:1). Jesus, the Son of God, and an integral part of the Triune Godhead, played a central role in the universe's creation: "All things were made through him, and without him was not anything made that was made" (John 1:3). Genesis 1:2 also acknowledges the Holy Spirit's role in creation.

God sustains all life. Colossians 1:16-17 elucidates about Jesus: "For by him all things were created, in heaven and on earth, visible and invisible, whether thrones or dominions or rulers or authorities—all things were created through him and for him. And he is before all things, and in him all things hold together."

God is actively engaged with humanity. Isaiah 46:9-10 proclaims, "I am God, and there is no other; I am God, and there is none like Me, declaring the end from the beginning and from ancient times things not yet done, saying, 'My counsel shall stand, and I will accomplish all my purpose.'"

God embodies love (1 John 4:8). His perfect love is manifested through Jesus, in His humility, service (Philippians 2:1-11), and particularly in sacrificing His life as atonement for our sins (John 15:13; 2 Corinthians 5:21). God completes love (1 Corinthians 13). Love is inseparable from God.

God is Triune. He is Father, Son, and Holy Spirit. Though God is one (Deuteronomy 6:4-5), He exists in three Persons, instructing His disciples to baptise in the name (singular) of the Father, Son, and Holy Spirit (Matthew 28:19-20). There is perfect unity and community within God Himself.

God is perfect in wisdom. He created everything and thus knows all that exists. Nothing surpasses His comprehension. Psalm 147:5 acknowledges, "Great is our Lord, and abundant in power; his understanding is beyond measure."

God is omnipresent. This signifies His existence everywhere at all times. Proverbs 15:3 states, "The eyes of the LORD are in every place, keeping watch on the evil and the good."

Psalm 139:7-10 reinforces, "Where shall I go from your Spirit? Or where shall I flee from your presence? If I ascend to heaven, you are there! If I make my bed in Sheol, you are there! If I take the wings of the morning and dwell in the uttermost parts of the sea, even there your hand shall lead me, and your right hand shall hold me."

Comprehending "what" God is entirely eludes human understanding. However, the revelation received incites worship, love, and service to the true, incomprehensible God.

Dear reader,
God is the ultimate creator and ruler of the universe, possessing attributes such as omnipotence, omniscience, and omnipresence.

Discovering the Identity of God - Question Activity

Objective: This activity aims to prompt personal reflection on the identity of God.

Instructions:

- Reflect on the question provided below.
- Write down your thoughts, feelings, and any insights that arise.
- Take your time and be sincere in your responses.
- After completing the activity, consider discussing your insights with a friend or mentor for further exploration.

Activity Question:

1. How would you describe the identity of God based on your understanding of His character, attributes, and interactions with humanity?

_____

_____

_____

Reflection:
Reflect on how your understanding of God shapes your beliefs, values, and relationship with Him.

DECLARED RIGHTEOUS:
Exploring the idea of justification

"Justification is not about making us good enough for God; it's about God declaring us righteous through the perfect sacrifice of Jesus Christ, covering us with His grace and love."- Nicholas Robertson

Justification means being declared righteous by God. It's an act where God pronounces a sinner as righteous because of that individual's faith in Christ. The crux of justification lies in God's declaration about the sinner, not in any internal change within the sinner. This declaration doesn't make someone holy; it merely deems them not guilty before God and consequently treated as holy. The actual journey toward holiness begins with sanctification, closely related to justification but distinct in definition.

A pivotal passage about justification for believers is found in Romans 3:21–26, highlighting that it's apart from the law, relying on faith in Jesus Christ. This righteousness isn't earned through rule-keeping but is a gift of grace received by faith in Christ's atonement through His blood. It's a testament to God's righteousness.

Several key aspects define justification:

- It's separate from the law, impossible to earn through works.
- It's made possible by Christ's sacrificial death, founded on His shed blood.
- It's a free gift from God to those who embrace Christ's sacrifice through faith.
- It displays God's righteousness.

Justification involves:

- Pardon from the penalty of sin, which is death.
- Restoration to God's favour, reestablishing a lost connection due to sin.
- The attribution of Christ's righteousness to believers' accounts, legally declaring them righteous.

We are justified, declared righteous, at the moment of our salvation. Christ finished the work required for our justification on the cross. This doesn't excuse, ignore, or endorse our sin; rather, it punishes our sin fully, with Christ serving as our substitute.

God's justification by grace through faith in Christ grants us peace with Him. It's akin to being divested of filthy clothes and adorned with the best robe. We're perceived as perfect and blameless by God and are encouraged to pursue goodness. Romans 5:18–19 in the Amplified Bible encapsulates the essence and outcome of justification, highlighting the contrast between Adam's sin and Christ's righteousness, ultimately bringing many into a state of righteousness and acceptance before God.

Dear reader,
Being justified by faith is foundational to the Christian faith, affirming that our standing with God is not based on our own actions or merits but is received as a gift through our trust in Jesus Christ. This principle highlights the transformative truth that our sins are forgiven, and we are declared righteous in God's sight through Christ's sacrificial death and resurrection. Through faith, we enter into a new covenant relationship with God, where His grace is abundant, and we are reconciled to Him. J

Exploring the Idea of Justification - Question Activity

Objective: This activity aims to prompt personal reflection on the concept of justification.

Instructions:

- Reflect on the question provided below.
- Write down your thoughts, feelings, and any insights that arise.
- Take your time and be sincere in your responses.
- After completing the activity, consider discussing your insights with a friend or mentor for further exploration.

Activity Question:

1. What does justification mean to you, and how do you understand its significance in the Christian faith?

_____

_____

_____

Reflection:
Consider your response and its implications for your spiritual journey. Reflect on how the concept of justification influences your understanding of God's grace and your relationship with Him. Think about how this understanding impacts your view of yourself and others. Consider how you can live in light of the truth of justification, embracing God's love and forgiveness, and extending grace to those around you.

THE SON OF GOD:
Understanding the Identity of Jesus Christ

"Jesus Christ is the eternal beacon of hope, the embodiment of God's unfailing love, and the ultimate source of redemption for all humanity."- Nicholas Robertson

The question of whether Jesus Christ existed is less debated compared to inquiries about His complete identity. While most agree on Jesus being a historical figure in Israel 2,000 years ago, discussions on His full essence spark debates. Various religions regard Jesus as a prophet, a revered teacher, or a righteous individual. However, the Bible portrays Jesus as far beyond those roles. C. S. Lewis, in "Mere Christianity," challenges the view of Jesus as merely a moral teacher, arguing that His claims cannot be confined to such a label. Lewis posits that Jesus was either the Son of God, a lunatic, or worse, but not merely a great human teacher (Macmillan, 1952, p. 55–56).

So, who did Jesus claim to be, and what does the Bible state about His identity? First and foremost, Jesus asserted His divinity. In John 10:30, He declared, "I and the Father are one." The Jews' reaction deemed this statement as blasphemous, perceiving it as Jesus claiming to be God (John

10:33). Despite this, Jesus never retracted His statement, implying equality with God.

Further affirmations of Jesus's divinity appear in John 8:58, where He claims pre-existence by referencing the name of God Himself, "I am" (Exodus 3:14). Moreover, biblical verses like John 1:1 and 1:14 assert that the Word was God and became flesh. Thomas referred to Jesus as "My Lord and my God" (John 20:28), unchallenged by Jesus. The apostles Paul and Peter also attributed divinity to Jesus in their writings.

The Old Testament contributes to affirming Jesus's deity through prophecies like Isaiah 9:6, designating the Messiah as the "Mighty God." Even God the Father testified to Jesus's identity as divine (Hebrews 1:8).

Why does Jesus's identity matter? Several reasons underline its significance:

- If Jesus is not God, it would cast doubt on His integrity and trustworthiness.
- The apostles' credibility would be in question if Jesus were not God.
- The Messiah, promised to be the "Holy One," necessitated God's incarnation as no human is inherently righteous.

- Jesus being God was crucial for His sacrificial death to atone for humanity's sins.
- Salvation requires Jesus to be God, as only God can be the Saviour (Hosea 13:4; 1 Timothy 2:3).

Jesus's dual nature as both God and man is essential. As God, He satisfied divine wrath, and as man, He had the capacity to die. As the Godman, Jesus serves as the perfect Mediator between heaven and earth. Salvation, according to Him, is solely attainable through faith in Jesus Christ as "the way, the truth, and the life" (John 14:6).

Dear reader,
Jesus is revered as the Son of God, the Messiah prophesied in ancient scriptures, and the Savior of humanity. His teachings of love, compassion, and forgiveness continue to inspire millions worldwide. Jesus' life, characterized by miraculous deeds, selflessness, and unwavering devotion to God's will, serves as a model of divine perfection and the ultimate example of humility and servanthood. His sacrificial death on the cross and subsequent resurrection offers hope of redemption and eternal life to all who believe in Him. Jesus is not only a historical figure but also a spiritual beacon, inviting individuals into a transformative relationship with God and guiding them towards spiritual enlightenment and fulfilment.

Understanding the Identity of Jesus Christ - Question Activity

Objective: This activity aims to prompt personal reflection on the identity of Jesus Christ.

Instructions:

- Reflect on the question provided below.
- Write down your thoughts, feelings, and any insights that arise.
- Take your time and be sincere in your responses.
- After completing the activity, consider discussing your insights with a friend, mentor, or fellow disciple for further exploration.

Activity Question:

1. Who is Jesus Christ to you, and how does your understanding of His identity impact your relationship with Him and your journey of discipleship?

_____

_____

_____

Reflection:

As you consider your response to the question, take time to contemplate the depth of Jesus' identity and its implications for your life as a disciple. Reflect on how your understanding of who Jesus is shapes your relationship with Him and your commitment to following His teachings.

THE DIVINE COMFORTER:
Exploring the Identity of the Holy Spirit

"The Holy Spirit is the divine guide, the gentle whisper in our hearts, leading us closer to God's truth and empowering us to live lives of faith and obedience."- Nicholas Robertson

Misconceptions surrounding the Holy Spirit abound, with some perceiving it as an enigmatic force or an impersonal power granted by God to Christ's followers. However, the Bible paints a clear picture of the Holy Spirit's identity—it unequivocally establishes the Holy Spirit as God and a divine being endowed with intellect, emotions, and volition.

Scripture explicitly designates the Holy Spirit as God, evident in Acts 5:3-4, where Peter confronts Ananias for deceiving the Holy Spirit, affirming that lying to the Spirit equates to lying to God. The Holy Spirit's divine attributes further solidify this truth. For instance, the Spirit's omnipresence is depicted in Psalm 139:7-8, acknowledging the Spirit's ubiquitous presence. Moreover, 1 Corinthians 2:10-11 reveals the Spirit's omniscience, delving into the profound depths of God's knowledge.

Additionally, the Holy Spirit embodies a distinct personality, possessing cognitive faculties, emotions, and a decisive will. Scripture illustrates the Spirit's ability to think and comprehend (1 Corinthians 2:10), expressing emotions like grief (Ephesians 4:30), and intervening on behalf of believers (Romans 8:26-27). Moreover, the Spirit exercises discretion according to His will (1 Corinthians 12:7-11).

As the third Person of the Trinity, the Holy Spirit assumes the role of the Comforter and Counsellor promised by Jesus (John 14:16, 26; 15:26), embodying the divine essence while fulfilling essential roles within the Godhead.

Gifts of the Holy Spirit

There exist three biblical compilations detailing the "gifts of the Spirit," also recognised as spiritual gifts. The primary passages outlining these spiritual gifts are Romans 12:6–8; 1 Corinthians 12:4–11; and 1 Corinthians 12:28. Another reference, Ephesians 4:11, lists church roles rather than spiritual gifts specifically. The spiritual gifts disclosed in Romans 12 encompass prophecy, serving, teaching, encouragement, giving, leadership, and mercy. Meanwhile, the list in 1 Corinthians 12:4–11 includes the word of wisdom, the word of knowledge, faith, healing, miraculous powers, prophecy, distinguishing between spirits, speaking in tongues, and interpretation of tongues. The list in 1

Corinthians 12:28 comprises healings, helps, governments, and diversities of tongues.

Let's delve into a brief elucidation of each gift:

- **Prophecy:** This gift entails speaking forth divine messages, encompassing the revelation of God's purposes, whether reproving the wicked, comforting the afflicted, or revealing hidden truths.
- **Serving:** Also referred to as "ministering," this gift embodies offering diverse forms of practical assistance to those in need.
- **Teaching:** It involves explaining and proclaiming God's Word, elucidating its significance and application to listeners' lives.
- **Encouraging:** This gift compels individuals to prompt others to follow God's truth, which may encompass correction, strengthening faith, or comforting in distress.
- **Giving:** Gifted givers joyfully share their possessions, extending financial, material, or personal support to those in need.
- **Leadership:** The gifted leader oversees and guides others within the church, steering with wisdom and grace, exhibiting the fruit of the Spirit.
- **Mercy:** Aligned with encouragement, this gift portrays compassion and sympathy, seeking to alleviate others' suffering in a cheerful manner.

- **Word of wisdom:** This gift involves articulating biblical truths skilfully, adeptly applying them to life circumstances with discernment.
- **Word of knowledge:** This gift comprehends truths revealed solely through divine revelation, encompassing the deep mysteries of God's Word.
- **Faith:** A gift available to all believers, it embodies unwavering confidence in God, His Word, promises, and the power of prayer.
- **Healing:** Though God continues to heal, this gift, primarily witnessed in apostolic times, entailed miraculous healing by individuals.
- **Miraculous powers:** A temporary sign gift involving supernatural events attributed to God's power.
- **Distinguishing (discerning) of spirits:** This gift discerns genuine messages of God from deceitful ones, safeguarding against deceptive doctrines.
- **Speaking in tongues:** This temporary gift enabled the preaching of the gospel across languages unknown to the speaker, affirming the message's divine origin.
- **Interpretation of tongues:** Gifted individuals could interpret the tongues spoken, communicating their message to others, ensuring understanding.
- **Helping:** This gift aids individuals in the church, extending assistance and compassion to those undergoing spiritual struggles.

Fruit of the Holy Spirit

Galatians 5:22-23 outlines the "fruit of the Spirit," which comprises attributes such as love, joy, peace, patience, kindness, goodness, faithfulness, gentleness, and self-control. This fruit is the evident outcome of the Holy Spirit's presence in a believer's life. The Bible emphasises that every individual receives the Holy Spirit upon believing in Jesus Christ (Romans 8:9; 1 Corinthians 12:13; Ephesians 1:13-14). An essential purpose of the Holy Spirit's arrival in a Christian's life is to initiate transformation. The Holy Spirit works to mould believers into the likeness of Christ, fostering traits that mirror His character. This contrast becomes evident when comparing the fruit of the Spirit to the behaviour's stemming from the sinful nature, as described in Galatians 5:19-21.

The passage in Galatians delineates behaviour's typifying those outside Christ, reflecting their inherent nature, while the fruit of the Spirit mirrors the nature of the Holy Spirit. The Christian journey involves a struggle between the sinful inclinations of our flesh and the new nature bestowed by Christ (2 Corinthians 5:17). As humans in a fallen state, we wrestle with desires that lean towards sinfulness (Romans 7:14-25). However, as Christians, we possess the Holy Spirit who not only produces His fruit within us but also empowers us to overcome the deeds of the sinful nature (2 Corinthians

5:17; Philippians 4:13). Though Christians may not consistently exhibit all the fruits of the Spirit, it remains a key objective in the Christian life to increasingly yield to the Holy Spirit's work, allowing His fruit to grow and flourish. This process involves the Holy Spirit triumphing over our contrary sinful desires. The display of the fruit of the Spirit aligns with God's desire for our lives, and through the Holy Spirit's guidance, it's an achievable goal.

How do I know what gift I possess?

Determining our spiritual gifts isn't a matter of uncovering a magic solution or taking a definitive test. The Holy Spirit is the distributor of these gifts, allocating them as He deems fit (1 Corinthians 12:7-11). It's a common challenge for Christians to solely focus on their perceived spiritual gifts, neglecting other areas of service. However, God calls us to serve Him wholeheartedly in all aspects of life. He equips us with the necessary gifts to fulfil His purposes.

Recognising our spiritual giftedness can be approached in diverse ways. Feedback from others observing our service to the Lord might reveal gifts we haven't recognised. Prayer is also pivotal. The Holy Spirit, the giver of these gifts, holds the precise knowledge of our spiritual endowments. Seeking guidance through prayer allows us to utilise these gifts for God's glory.

Certainly, God assigns specific roles and grants corresponding gifts, like teaching or serving. Yet, knowing our spiritual gift isn't an excuse to limit our service exclusively to that area. While it's beneficial to understand our spiritual gifts, over-focusing on them can cause us to overlook other opportunities to serve God. When our devotion is to serve God, He provides the necessary spiritual gifts for our service.

Dear reader,
The Holy Spirit, often referred to as the third person of the Trinity in Christian theology, is a divine presence that permeates the believer's life with guidance, comfort, and empowerment. Described in Scripture as the advocate promised by Jesus to His disciples, the Holy Spirit serves as a constant companion, offering wisdom and discernment in navigating life's challenges. Beyond mere guidance, the Holy Spirit is believed to indwell believers, transforming hearts and empowering them to live out the teachings of Jesus. This divine presence is also credited with equipping believers with spiritual gifts, such as prophecy, healing, and speaking in tongues, to edify the church and fulfil God's purposes on earth. As believers yield to the Holy Spirit's leading, they experience a deepening intimacy with God and a newfound boldness in sharing the love and truth of Christ with others.

THE MYSTERY OF THREE IN ONE:
Exploring the Concept of the Trinity

"The Trinity embodies the unity of God in three distinct persons—Father, Son, and Holy Spirit—reflecting a divine harmony and love that beckons us into communion with the Triune God."- Nicholas Robertson

The Trinity, a core aspect of Christian faith, is a deeply intricate concept that surpasses human comprehension. It encompasses the belief in one God existing as three distinct Persons—the Father, the Son (Jesus), and the Holy Spirit—while being unified as a single divine entity. Although the term "Trinity" is not explicitly mentioned in the Bible, the scriptures offer substantial support for this doctrine.

The Bible consistently emphasises the singularity of God (Deuteronomy 6:4; 1 Corinthians 8:4; Galatians 3:20; 1 Timothy 2:5). Within the Trinity, there are three distinct Persons: the Father, the Son, and the Holy Spirit. While the exact term may not be present in scripture, various passages (Genesis 1:1, 26; 3:22; 11:7; Isaiah 6:8, 48:16, 61:1; Matthew 3:16-17, 28:19; 2 Corinthians 13:14) imply a multiplicity within God. The Bible portrays different Persons of the

Trinity as separate entities. In the Old Testament, distinctions between "LORD" and "Lord" imply this division within God (Genesis 19:24; Hosea 1:4). Jesus' conversations with the Father indicate a clear differentiation between them (John 14:16-17).

Each member of the Trinity is acknowledged as God in various scriptures (John 1:1, 14; Acts 5:3-4; Romans 9:5; Hebrews 1:8). Scripture reveals a hierarchical structure within the Trinity, signifying roles without diminishing their divine equality. The Holy Spirit and the Son are depicted as subservient to the Father, illustrating a distinctive order within their unity (John 14:16).

the concept of the Trinity is indeed central to Christian theology, encapsulating the belief in one God who exists in three distinct persons: the Father, the Son (Jesus Christ), and the Holy Spirit. The Nicene Creed, formulated in the 4th century, is one of the most widely accepted statements of Christian faith, affirming this belief in the triune nature of God. Each person of the Trinity plays a unique role in the life of believers and in the narrative of salvation as depicted in the Bible.

The Father, Son and Holy Spirit is depicted in Nicene Creed:

"We believe in one God, the Father the Almighty ... We believe in one Lord Jesus Christ, the only Son of God ... We believe in the Holy Spirit, the Lord and giver of life."— The Nicene Creed

How can God simultaneously be three and one? It's crucial to grasp that God is one yet also manifests as three distinct persons.

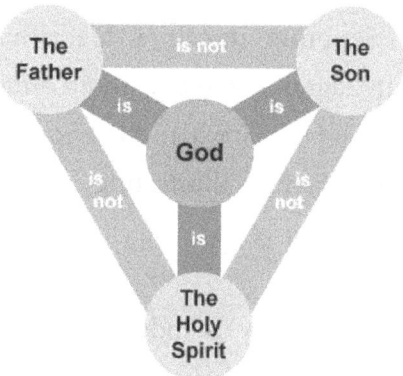

Dear reader,

The Bible describes God as three separate individuals functioning as one: not one person with three different roles. One such account is captured by Matthew:

As soon as Jesus was baptised, he went up out of the water. At that moment heaven was opened, and he saw the Spirit of God descending like a dove and alighting on him. And a voice from heaven said, 'This is my Son, whom I love; with him I am well pleased.'— Matthew 3:16–17

THE COMMUNITY OF BELIEVERS:
Investigating the Identity of the Church

"The church is not merely a building; it is a living, breathing community of believers, united by faith, bound by love, and called to shine the light of Christ in a dark world."- Nicholas Robertson

The perception of the church as merely a physical structure doesn't align with its biblical definition. The term "church" translates from the Greek word "ekklesia," signifying "an assembly" or "called-out ones." Its essence isn't rooted in a building but in people. Ironically, when asked about their church, many often point to a physical place. Romans 16:5 highlights a church meeting in a house—a gathering of believers, not a dedicated edifice.

The church represents the body of Christ, with Him as the head (Ephesians 1:22–23). It comprises all believers from Pentecost (Acts 2) until Christ's return, seen in two aspects: the universal church and the local church.

The universal church includes every individual worldwide with a personal relationship with Jesus Christ. "For we were all baptised by one Spirit into one body—whether Jews or Greeks, slave or free—and we were all given the one Spirit to drink" (1 Corinthians 12:13). It comprises all who have embraced salvation through faith in Christ.

The local church, as seen in Galatians 1:1–2, existed in various regions, like Galatia, encompassing multiple local bodies of believers. These are distinct entities like Baptist, Lutheran, or E-Free churches, representing localised fellowships. These local gatherings are where believers express the communal aspects described in 1 Corinthians 12—nurturing, guiding, and strengthening each other in Christ.

Dear reader,
The church isn't a structure or a denomination. Biblically, it's the collective body of Christ—those who have embraced Christ for salvation. Local churches are gatherings of individuals professing faith in Christ. The genuineness of one's faith determines their membership in the universal church. Local church gatherings foster the application of principles, nurturing spiritual growth and mutual support among believers.

LIVING IN VICTORY:
Embracing Your Identity in Christ

"Embracing your identity in Christ is not about becoming someone new, but discovering who you were always meant to be—forgiven, redeemed, and deeply loved by God."- Nicholas Robertson

Our identity, rooted in Christ, is a testament to newness. As per 2 Corinthians 5:17, we're fashioned anew in Christ. Identity, defined as the set of distinctive characteristics defining something, should manifest the newness in Christ both within us and to the world. Just as being "in the world" is conspicuous, being "in Christ" should be equally discernible. Our identity as "Christians" denotes "followers of Christ."

In our fresh identity in Christ, we cease being slaves to sin (Romans 6:6) and embrace reconciliation with God (Romans 5:10). This transformative identity reshapes our connection with God, family, and our perception of the world. In Christ, we assume a relationship akin to His with God—we become His children. God, in His embrace, adopts us as sons, enabling us to call Him "Abba! Father!" (Romans 8:15–16). We are co-heirs (Galatians 3:29) and friends (John 15:15) of

Christ. This bond transcends even earthly familial ties (Matthew 10:35–37). Instead of fear, we approach God as our Father, confidently seeking His guidance and wisdom (Hebrews 4:16; James 1:5), reassured that nothing can sever our connection with Him (Romans 8:38–39). Our obedience becomes an expression of trust, a pivotal aspect in our closeness to Him (John 14:23).

The family of God encompasses a diverse assembly of believers striving towards deeper communion with God (1 Corinthians 12:13). It's a cohesive unit, bolstered by the unique contributions of each member (Romans 12:6–8). Within this family, members strive for each other's well-being (1 Corinthians 10:24), offering encouragement (Galatians 6:1–2) and forgiveness (Matthew 18:21–22). Every member has a distinct role, upheld with respect and grace (1 Peter 5:1–5). Love—selfless, sacrificial—is the defining thread among them, mirroring the agape love of God who sacrificed for us (Galatians 2:20).

We've transitioned from worldly citizenship to belonging to a heavenly, God-governed kingdom (2 Corinthians 6:14—7:1). The allure of earthly pursuits no longer captivates us (Colossians 3:2). Earthly sufferings and trials no longer overshadow us, nor do we prize worldly values (Colossians 1:24; 1 Peter 3:14; 4:12–14; 1 Timothy 6:9–11). Our transformed bodies and actions demonstrate a mind no longer conformed to the world but committed to God's righteousness (Romans 12:1–2; Romans 6:13). Our new perspective unveils the spiritual battle, recognising our foe as spiritual forces impeding people from God (Ephesians 6:12).This paints the portrait of a mature Christ-follower. Our identity in Christ extends the grace to grow into spiritual maturity, a journey reflecting our new identity (Philippians 1:6). Life, rooted in our identity in Christ, resonates with the presence of a loving Father, an expansive familial embrace, and an understanding that we belong to a heavenly realm, disassociated from earthly confines.

Dear reader,
Our new identity in Christ is a profound transformation that occurs when we accept Him as our Savior. In this divine exchange, our old self, with its sin and brokenness, is crucified with Christ, and we are born anew as children of God. Through His redemptive work on the cross, Jesus not only forgives our sins but also clothes us in His righteousness, restoring our relationship with God and granting us access to His abundant grace.

THE HEART OF SERVICE:
Exploring the Meaning of Servanthood

"Servanthood is not about seeking recognition or accolades, but about humbly using our gifts and talents to serve others, reflecting the love and compassion of our Servant-King, Jesus Christ."

The core principle of servanthood, deeply embedded in the Bible's narrative, finds its zenith in the life and teachings of Jesus Christ—the quintessential Servant of all. His profound words, "For even the Son of Man did not come to be served, but to serve, and to give His life a ransom for many" (Mark 10:45), exemplify the heart of true servanthood.

In understanding servanthood, one inevitably encounters Jesus Christ, the epitome of servanthood. His life was a paragon of selfless service, emphasising that true leadership resides in servitude. Despite His divine stature, Christ chose to empty Himself, assuming the form of a servant, setting an unparalleled example of humility and service (Philippians 2:6-7). His life modelled a servant's heart—one that doesn't grasp for position but delights in selfless acts of love and care.

The New Testament underscores the essence of ministry as servanthood—service rendered in love. This principle encapsulates the core of Christian living, emphasising that all believers are called to ministry, embodying the role of servants for the glory of God (Matthew 28:18-20). It accentuates the profound reality that living is indeed giving, any other pursuit reeks of self-centredness and ennui.

General Bruce C. Clarke, astutely notes, "Rank is given to you to enable you to better serve those above and below you. It is not given for you to practice your idiosyncrasies." This sentiment resonates deeply with the biblical perspective of servanthood—one that sees position and authority as avenues to better serve, rather than self-aggrandisement.

Servanthood finds its ultimate purpose in serving Christ Himself. Every action, every service rendered to others, is a service to Christ (Colossians 3:23-24). Just as God the Father served humanity by sacrificing Christ on the cross, believers are called to serve others selflessly, offering the Gospel and their lives as a testament to this sacrificial service (1 Thessalonians 1:5-6).

Christ's teaching, "Whoever desires to become great among you, let him be your servant" (Matthew 20:26), elucidates the paradox of greatness in God's kingdom—found in humble service. The pursuit of greatness in the Kingdom of God is inextricably linked with the heart of a servant—one who embodies selflessness and compassion in serving others.

Dear reader,

The journey toward embracing the heart of a servant begins with understanding and imbibing the life and teachings of Jesus Christ—the ultimate Servant. Servanthood, a foundational aspect of Christian living, permeates every facet of life, compelling believers to mirror Christ's humility and sacrificial love in their service to others.

WALKING IN TRANSPARENCY:
Understanding the Importance of Accountability

"Accountability is the courageous commitment to stand in the light of truth, allowing others to speak into our lives, guide us towards growth, and keep us aligned with our values and goals." – Nicholas Robertson

In a world rife with temptation and constant spiritual warfare, many Christians seek an "accountability partner" to navigate these challenges alongside them. Having a trusted brother or sister in Christ to share the burdens of temptation and pray together is invaluable. Even King David, in solitude, succumbed to temptation when Satan led him into adultery with Bathsheba (2 Samuel 11). Scripture reminds us that our struggle is not against flesh and blood but against spiritual forces (Ephesians 6:12). Recognising the battle against the forces of darkness, it's essential to gather support around us. Making ourselves accountable to a fellow believer can be a source of encouragement and aid in our fight. Paul urges us to equip ourselves with the full armour of God to stand firm in the face of evil (Ephesians 6:13). Anticipating temptations and being prepared is crucial.

Satan is well-versed in exploiting our vulnerabilities. He strikes when we're most susceptible—during marital strife, in the aftermath of discipline, or amid difficulties at work. At such moments, where do we turn for help? We desire to honour God, yet our strength wanes. Proverbs 27:17 illustrates the importance of companionship: "Iron sharpens iron, and one man sharpens another." A friend's encouragement and support are often the missing pieces in battling against Satan's wiles.

The writer of Hebrews emphasises the significance of mutual encouragement and support within the Body of Christ, urging believers not to neglect meeting together but to spur each other toward love and good deeds (Hebrews 10:24–25). James also hints at the value of accountability through confession and prayer for healing (James 5:16).

Dear reader,

An accountability partner can play a pivotal role in the journey to conquer sin. They can offer encouragement, correction, guidance, share in joys and sorrows, and stand by your side in prayer and confession. Therefore, every Christian should consider having an accountability partner—a trusted confidant with whom they can pray, talk, and share their struggles.

THE POWER OF YIELDING:
Understanding the Joy of Submission

"Submission is not weakness; it is the courageous act of surrendering our will to God's, trusting in His wisdom and sovereignty to lead us on the path of righteousness."- Nicholas Robertson

The Bible emphatically advocates the submission and reverence to authority figures. This doctrine, however, poses a challenging concept for many, as it seemingly endorses those who wield power in a harsh or unjust manner. One of the most frequently cited passages in this regard comes from Romans 13, where God instructs believers to yield to "governing authorities, for there is no authority except that which God has established" (Romans 13:1). Rebelling against such authority is equated to rebelling against God Himself (Romans 13:2).

Certain quarters argue that such directives refer only to benevolent rulers, as the Scripture goes on to say that these rulers "hold no terror for those who do right" and are "God's servant, an agent of wrath to bring punishment on the wrongdoer." This underscores the necessity to submit and pay taxes since these authorities are "God's servants, who give their full time to governing" (Romans 13:3-6).

But how does God advise reacting to unjust rulers? In another significant yet challenging passage, the Bible calls upon slaves to submit themselves to their masters, not only to those who are considerate but also to those who are harsh. Further clarifying, it states, "For it is God's will that by doing good, you should silence the ignorant talk of foolish men" and encourages showing respect to everyone, loving fellow believers, fearing God, and honouring the king. Enduring unjust suffering is commended, aligning with Christ's example (1 Peter 2:15, 17-21). These profound messages might provoke the perception that God is inclined towards sadism. However, this interpretation would be a misreading of the Bible. God's consistent call to exhibit love, honour, and respect reflects His vision for His Kingdom on earth. He desires us to live life abundantly (John 10:10) and promises a glorious and eternal life (John 3:16; 14:2-3, 23).

Ephesians 6:6-9 underscores the need to obey not merely to win favour when observed by others but as "slaves of Christ, doing the will of God from your heart." Serving wholeheartedly as if serving the Lord is emphasised, promising rewards for good deeds. This message extends to slave masters, urging them to treat their slaves likewise since God is the master of both (Ephesians 6:6-9).

Despite instances of poor or tyrannical governance, as evident in biblical accounts and today's world, God assures us that respect, kindness, and submission align with His plan (1 Thessalonians 5:12-18). Failure to adhere to this precept results in a descent into depravity and anarchy due to self-centredness (2 Timothy 3:1-9). God assures believers that transient challenges should never overshadow the euphoric ecstasy that awaits them in His divine presence.

Dear reader,
True joy is found in relinquishing control and allowing God to work in and through us, knowing that His purposes are always for our ultimate good and His glory. Submission is not about passivity or resignation but rather about actively aligning our hearts with God's will and participating in His divine plan with a spirit of humility and obedience. As we submit ourselves to God, we experience the freedom and peace that come from living in harmony with His design for our lives, and we find joy in knowing that we are walking in His perfect will. Submitting to others becomes easier when we first submit to God.

CULTIVATING DISCIPLINE:
Navigating the Path to Spiritual Growth

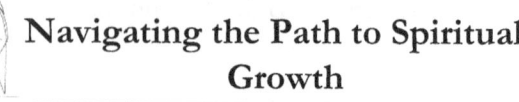

"Discipline is the bridge between goals and accomplishment, the unwavering commitment to daily actions that align with our deepest values and aspirations." – Nicholas Robertson

One of the biggest hurdles many of us face is mastering self-control—being able to resist indulging in things we ought not to and actively pursuing beneficial habits. These can range from mundane, like managing food, exercise, or sleep, to moral, such as maintaining a cool temper, resisting falsehoods, or practising virtues like temperance and integrity.

Discipline embodies the virtue of exercising self-control, a fruit of the spirit, central in the Bible. While often linked with raising children, the Bible primarily underscores a believer's journey to mirror Jesus Christ. It grows through sanctification by the Holy Spirit, fostering a physically and spiritually sound life for Christians.

According to Merriam-Webster's dictionary, discipline, as a noun, refers to "control gained by enforcing obedience or order; orderly or prescribed conduct or pattern of behaviour; self-control." As a verb, it means "to train or develop by instruction and exercise especially in self-control; to bring a group under control." It may also imply punishment due to rule breaking. In the Bible, it serves two purposes.

In the book of Proverbs, discipline is mostly about well-being. It's about practising self-control regarding food, drink, curbing lust, and attending to crucial life aspects. The woman portrayed in Proverbs 31, embodying a good wife and wise living, exemplifies this kind of discipline:

"She rises while it is yet night and provides food for her household and portions for her maidens. She considers a field and buys it; with the fruit of her hands, she plants a vineyard. She dresses herself with strength and makes her arms strong. She perceives that her merchandise is profitable. Her lamp does not go out at night. She puts her hands to the distaff, and her hands hold the spindle" (Proverbs 31:15-19).

In the New Testament, while virtues and self-control are significant, the focus shifts to spiritual discipline. It's about growing in the fruits of the spirit and avoiding sin. The Apostle Paul, in a letter to the church in Galatia, succinctly explains this concept: "But the fruit of the Spirit is love, joy, peace, patience, kindness, goodness, faithfulness, gentleness, self-control; against such things there is no law" (Galatians 5:18-23).

Sin makes it tough for people to turn from the works of the flesh and emulate Christ, but the Holy Spirit aids believers in growing in discipline and Christ-like characteristics.

In the Bible, discipline encompasses moral training, instruction, correction fostering spiritual growth, character development, and Christian maturity. Proverbs highlights the wisdom in embracing discipline humbly for a fulfilling and successful life. God's discipline might sometimes come in the form of punishment or trials, yet it's rooted in His love and concern for our well-being.

The Hebrew and Greek words translated as "discipline" in the Bible signify "instruction, training, rebuke, reproof, warning, and correction." Discipline forms a crucial part of the spiritual journey of the church and every Jesus follower. Christian discipleship involves a lifelong process of emulating Jesus and His way of life.

The Scriptures encourage believers to embrace God's discipline and anticipate it. Those who accept the Lord's discipline find joy and completeness. Corrective discipline is identified as the pathway to life, and the Bible speaks significantly to parents about guiding and correcting their children.

Dear reader,

Cultivating spiritual discipline is a transformative journey of deepening one's relationship with the divine. It involves intentional practices and habits aimed at nurturing the soul and aligning oneself with the will of God. Spiritual discipline encompasses a wide range of activities, including prayer, meditation, scripture study, worship, fasting, and service to others. These practices serve to cultivate a heart of humility, gratitude, and reverence, fostering spiritual growth and maturity.

BEARING WITNESS:
Understanding the Power of a Christian Testimony

"A Christian testimony is not just a story; it's a living testament to the transformative power of God's love, grace, and redemption in our lives."- Nicholas Robertson

The term "testimony" carries diverse connotations. In some scenarios, it involves solemn declarations in a courtroom under oath, recounting personal experiences or knowledge relevant to a case. When we marry "Christian" to "testimony," it refines the scope to a particular narrative exclusive to those who have found solace in Christ's forgiveness.

A Christian testimony narrates the profound journey of encountering the God of the Bible, catalysed by the Holy Spirit's divine intervention in our hearts. It encapsulates the narrative of how we, as believers, embraced Christianity, often influenced by pivotal events orchestrated by God's miraculous touch. Though the clarity of these moments often crystallises in hindsight, their sharing is pivotal in our spiritual journey. However, while our conversion story holds significance, the core of a Christian testimony should pivot on the crux of the Gospel—the death, resurrection, and burial of Christ.

This testimony transcends the mere tale of our conversion; it delves into the sanctifying work of the Lord in our lives post-conversion. It encompasses how the Lord guided us through tumultuous times, be it grievous losses or profound illnesses, nurturing and fortifying our faith in Him. Crucially, it should articulate the ongoing process wherein the Spirit, now residing within us, moulds us into mature, devout Christians. The spotlight remains on the Lord and His faithfulness throughout, interspersed with scriptural references that echo His unwavering nature (Psalm 18:2, 6).

Dear reader,
A Christian testimony isn't just a narrative; it's a testament to the transformative power of encountering Christ, unveiling His continual presence and guidance in our lives.

Sharing a Christian testimony brings about numerous benefits, both for the individual sharing and for those who hear it. Firstly, sharing your testimony allows for personal reflection and deepening of faith as the individual recalls and recounts the ways in which God has worked in your life. It serves as a reminder of God's faithfulness, grace, and provision, strengthening the believer's trust and reliance on Him. Additionally, sharing a testimony provides encouragement and inspiration to others who may be facing similar struggles or seeking answers to spiritual questions. By hearing real-life examples of God's transformative power, listeners are uplifted, challenged, and motivated to pursue their own relationship with God. Furthermore, sharing testimonies fosters unity and connection within the Christian community, as believers come together to celebrate God's work in their lives and support one another on their journey of faith. Ultimately, the benefits of sharing a Christian testimony extend beyond individual lives, serving as a powerful tool for spreading the Gospel and bringing glory to God.

Years ago, I met a young man in the lush hills of Jamaica named Jamal on a Christian camp. During one of our interactions, he shared with me the impact of someone's testimony on his own journey to becoming a Christian. Below is an excerpt:

I spent my days working hard in the fields, tending to the crops that sustained my family and my village. Yet, despite my toil, I felt a deep emptiness in my heart.

One day, as I rested beneath the shade of a mango tree, an old friend named Tanya approached me with a joyful glow about her. Tanya had recently become a Christian, and her newfound faith radiated from her like the Caribbean sun.

Curious, I asked Tanya why she had chosen to become a Christian. With a warm smile, Tanya shared her story of how she had once felt lost and without purpose, but through Jesus Christ, she found hope, forgiveness, and a new life filled with joy and peace.

Intrigued by Tanya's words, I began to ponder my own life and the longing I felt deep within his soul. I realised that despite my hard work and the beauty of my homeland, something was missing. I yearned for the same sense of peace and purpose that Tanya had found in her faith.

With a newfound determination, I decided to explore Christianity for myself. I attended church services, read the Bible, and prayed earnestly to God. As I explored the teachings of Jesus Christ, I discovered the truth that had eluded me for so long: that true fulfilment and eternal life could only be found in a relationship with God through Jesus Christ.

Transformed by my newfound faith, I embraced Christianity wholeheartedly. I found forgiveness for my past mistakes, strength for my daily struggles, and a community of believers who supported and encouraged me along the way.

From that day forward, my life took on new meaning and purpose. I no longer felt lost or alone, for I am convinced that I am loved by a God who had a plan for my life. And as I shared my own story of faith with others, I became a beacon of hope and inspiration to others, showing them the way to true happiness and fulfilment in Jesus Christ.

CRAFTING YOUR STORY:
A Guide to Sharing Your Testimony

"Crafting a testimony is not about perfect words or eloquent speeches; it's about authentically sharing the story of God's faithfulness and grace in our lives, so that others may be inspired by His transformative power."- Nicholas Robertson

Crafting an impactful testimony involves blending your personal journey with the essence of the Gospel of Christ. It's about articulating your experience in a way that communicates the path to salvation for someone else. Start by meticulously jotting down the particulars of your transformative encounter with Christ. This isn't just about the 'what'; it delves into the 'how' and 'when' of your spiritual awakening. Consider pivotal questions like who introduced you to Christ, the events that steered you towards trust in Him, the moment you embraced faith, the setting where this epiphany unfolded, and the subsequent blessings your newfound faith bestowed upon your life. Once you've gathered these elements, craft them into a flowing narrative. Aim for concise storytelling; strive to encapsulate your testimony within three minutes or less, making it easily shareable and impactful. But don't overlook the power of Scripture in your testimony. The authority of your words derives from the Word of God. Integrate appropriate Scriptures to underpin your experience. Your testimony should revolve around realising your separation from God due to sin (Romans 3:23), the consequential awareness of eternal separation from God (Romans 6:23), the profound revelation of God sending His flawless Son, Jesus, to atone for your sins (Romans 5:8), and the pivotal act of receiving forgiveness solely through faith in Christ's sacrifice (Acts 16:31). The potency of your testimony lies not just in recounting your narrative but in intertwining it with the eternal truths encapsulated in Scripture. As you shape your testimony, ensure that it reflects the transformative power of your personal journey intertwined with the unwavering truths of the Gospel.

Below is a guide for crafting and sharing your testimony for greater impact:

Introduction:

Dear brothers and sisters in Christ, today I am humbled and grateful to share with you my personal journey of faith and the transformative work that God has done in my life. It is my prayer that my testimony will encourage and inspire each of you in your own walk with the Lord, reminding us of all His unfailing love, grace, and power to bring about redemption and renewal.

Before Christ:

- *Begin by briefly sharing about your life before encountering Jesus Christ.*
- *This could include experiences of emptiness, struggles, or searching for meaning and purpose.*

Encounter with Christ:

- *Describe the moment or series of events when you encountered Jesus Christ.*
- *Share how you came to know Him personally as your Lord and Saviour.*
- *This could involve a specific event, a conversation, or a period of spiritual seeking.*

Transformation:

- *Reflect on the ways in which your life has been transformed by your relationship with Jesus Christ.*
- *Share examples of how His love, forgiveness, and grace have impacted your attitudes, behaviours, and relationships.*

Challenges and Growth:

- *Acknowledge the challenges or trials you have faced as a Christian and how God has been faithful to sustain you through them.*

- *Share about moments of doubt, fear, or uncertainty, and how God's Word and the support of other believers helped you grow in faith.*

Victories and Blessings:

- *Celebrate the victories and blessings that God has bestowed upon you since becoming a Christian.*
- *Share about answered prayers, moments of spiritual breakthrough, or experiences of His provision and guidance.*

Current Walk with God:

- *Describe your current relationship with God and how you continue to grow in your faith.*
- *Share about your practices of prayer, Bible study, worship, and service to others.*

Call to Action:

- *Encourage your listeners to consider their own relationship with Jesus Christ and to reflect on how God is working in their lives.*
- *Invite them to respond to the Gospel and to open their hearts to receive His love and grace.*

Conclusion:

Dear friends, as I conclude my testimony, I want to thank each of you for listening with open hearts. May we all continue to walk in the light of God's truth, grace, and love, shining brightly for His glory and leading others to know the saving power of Jesus Christ. Amen.

Dear reader,

Sharing your testimony boldly is an act of courage and vulnerability that can have a profound impact on both you and others. It involves openly sharing your personal journey of faith, including the struggles, doubts, and victories you've experienced along the way. By sharing your story, you not only bear witness to the transformative power of God in your life but also offer hope and encouragement to those who may be facing similar challenges. Boldly sharing your testimony requires stepping out of your comfort zone and trusting in the guiding presence of the Holy Spirit. It means overcoming fear of judgment or rejection and boldly proclaiming the faithfulness of God in your life. When you share your testimony boldly, you invite others to encounter the love and grace of God and inspire them to seek a deeper relationship with Him.

BEARING WITNESS:
Sharing Your Testimony with Boldness and Grace

"Your testimony is not just your story; it's a powerful tool for God to use in the lives of others, revealing His love, grace, and faithfulness."- Nicholas Robertson

Every time you share your story of how you came to have a personal relationship with God, you give honour and glory to God, which pleases Him. That story is your Christian testimony: the tale of how God transformed your life through a personal relationship with Him.

Your testimony, no matter how ordinary or extraordinary you perceive it to be, is a narrative about God's character. It's your firsthand account of how God rescued you from sin and death through Christ, bringing about a change in your life. When you share your story with others, you enable them to understand what God is like and what He can do.

How to prepare your Personal Testimony?

Whether you're in a queue at the grocery store, spending time with a family member, or standing in front of a group of people, the Bible encourages you to "always be ready" to explain your hope in Christ with gentleness and respect (1

Peter 3:15-16). Your story is one of the most valuable tools you have for sharing the gospel with someone who doesn't follow Jesus. And it's not a tool you need to remember to carry in your backpack or purse; it's something you always possess, no matter the situation. Being ready to share your story when an opportunity arises is crucial if you're faithful about sharing the story God has given you. You might think that because it's your story, you don't have to do anything to be prepared to tell it. After all, you were there when it happened, and you're living it now. As Christians, we don't merely tell our story because it's "the right thing to do." We do it because it's biblical and because God works when we take steps of faith to share with others.

The Bible recounts various instances where people shared how God transformed their lives. One of the most well-known testimonies is from the apostle Paul. Paul transitioned from persecuting Christians to following Jesus, establishing churches, and contributing to over half of the New Testament. Consider his testimony before a crowd in Acts 22:1-21 to understand the essential components of telling your story.

- **Paul starts with a brief account of his life (Acts 22: 1-3)**

"Brothers and fathers, listen now to my defence." When they heard him speak to them in Aramaic, they became very quiet. Then Paul

said: "I am a Jew, born in Tarsus of Cilicia, but brought up in this city. I studied under Gamaliel and was thoroughly trained in the law of our ancestors. I was just as zealous for God as any of you are today."

- **Paul describes his life before Christ (Acts 22: 4-5)**

"I persecuted the followers of this Way to their death, arresting both men and women and throwing them into prison, as the high priest and all the Council can themselves testify. I even obtained letters from them to their associates in Damascus and went there to bring these people as prisoners to Jerusalem to be punished."

- **Paul explains how he came to know Christ (Acts 22: 6-13)**

"About noon as I came near Damascus, suddenly a bright light from heaven flashed around me. I fell to the ground and heard a voice say to me, 'Saul! Saul! Why do you persecute me?' "'Who are You, Lord?' I asked. "'I am Jesus of Nazareth, whom you are persecuting,' He replied. My companions saw the light, but they did not understand the voice of Him who was speaking to me. "'What shall I do, Lord?' I asked. "'Get up,' the Lord said, 'and go into Damascus. There you will be told all that you have been assigned to do.' My companions led me by the hand into Damascus because the brilliance of the light had blinded me. "A man named Ananias came to see me. He was a devout observer of the law and highly respected by all the Jews living there. He stood beside me and said, 'Brother Saul, receive your sight!' And at that very moment I was able to see him."

- **Paul speaks about his life after encountering Christ (Acts 22: 14-18)**

"Then [Ananias] said: 'The God of our ancestors has chosen you to know His will and to see the Righteous One and to hear words from His mouth. You will be His witness to all people of what you have seen and heard. And now what are you waiting for? Get up, be baptised, and wash your sins away, calling on His name.' "When I returned to Jerusalem and was praying at the temple, I fell into a trance and saw the Lord speaking to me. 'Quick!' He said 'Leave Jerusalem immediately, because the people here will not accept your testimony about Me.'"

- **Paul concludes with his obedience to Christ (Acts 22: 19-21)**

"'Lord,' I replied, 'these people know that I went from one synagogue to another to imprison and beat those who believe in You. And when the blood of your martyr Stephen was shed, I stood there giving my approval and guarding the clothes of those who were killing Him.' "Then the Lord said to me, 'Go; I will send you far away to the Gentiles.'"

Lessons from Paul's Testimony

Having carefully examined Paul's testimony, we have a better understanding of a good framework for telling our story. As you prepare to share, consider these five elements of a personal testimony. As you go through this list, jot down your answers to the questions in each section.

- **The Beginning**

Identify a theme that you can use to frame your story. What was the focal point of your life (e.g. relationships, reputation, success) that God used to guide you towards Him? Briefly illustrate how that influenced your life.

- **Your Life Before Christ**

Portray what your life was like before you came to Christ. Don't dwell excessively on, or boast about, past sins. Share only the details that relate to your theme, just enough to reveal your need for Christ. Reflect on these questions:

- ✓ What aspect of my life before Christ will resonate most with the non-Christians I know?
- ✓ What was the central focus of my life?
- ✓ Where did I derive my security, identity, or happiness from?
- ✓ How did those things start to disappoint me?

- **How You Came to Christ**

Provide details about why and how you became a Christian. Communicate in a manner that both the person you are talking to and anyone who overhears can understand how they can become a Christian too. Even if your listeners aren't ready for that, your story and explanation of the gospel might draw them to God in the future. Ponder these questions:

- ✓ When did I first hear the gospel?
- ✓ How did I initially react?
- ✓ When and why did my perception of Christ start to change?
- ✓ What were the final struggles I faced before accepting Him?
- ✓ Why did I ultimately decide to accept Christ (or surrender my life entirely to Him)?

- **Your Life After Coming to Christ**

Share some of the changes Christ has brought about in your life related to your theme. Highlight changes in your character, attitude, or outlook, not just changes in behaviour. Be realistic. Even as Christians, we still face challenges. Life isn't perfect, but what's different about your life now?

Dear reader,
Remember to share your Christian tale boldly.

COMMUNING WITH GOD:
Unveiling the Purpose of Prayer

"Prayer is the soul's sincere desire, expressed in words or in silence, lifting us into the presence of God and anchoring us in His peace and grace." – Nicholas Robertson

The simplest definition of prayer is "communication with God." It's not passive reflection but a direct conversation with the Creator. Through prayer, believers in Jesus Christ express emotions, desires, and foster fellowship with God.

Prayer can take various forms, audible or silent, private, or public, formal, or informal. Yet, every prayer must stem from faith (James 1:6), be offered in the name of Jesus Christ (John 16:23) and be empowered by the Holy Spirit (Romans 8:26). The International Standard Bible Encyclopaedia defines Christian prayer as communication addressed to God as Father, through Christ as Mediator, and by the enabling grace of the indwelling Spirit.

The wicked lack the desire to pray (Psalm 10:4), but God's children naturally incline toward prayer (Luke 11:1). Scripture describes prayer as seeking God's favour, pouring out one's soul, crying out to heaven, drawing near to God, and kneeling before the Father.

Paul instructs believers not to be anxious but to present their requests to God in prayer and thanksgiving, promising God's peace that surpasses understanding (Philippians 4:6–7). Essentially, God desires believers to bring everything to Him in prayer—maintaining an ongoing conversation with God throughout the day.

How often should one pray?

The Bible advises "pray without ceasing" (1 Thessalonians 5:17). Some find structures like the ACTS (Adoration, Confession, Thanksgiving and Supplication) formula helpful, but there's no set formula for prayer. The key is simply engaging in it. Prayer is a way to deepen our relationship with God, displaying our trust and complete dependence on Him.

Through prayer, Christians communicate their praise, gratitude, love for God, share their lives, make requests, seek guidance, and ask for wisdom. It's a vital connection with God, demonstrating love and trust. Prayer isn't about imposing our will but aligning ourselves with God's will (1 John 5:14–15; James 4:3). In essence, it's saying, "Not my will, but Yours be done." Answered prayer comes from aligning with God's will and Word. Prayer, at its core, is simple—our direct line to God.

Dear reader,

For more information on prayer, consider acquiring this book: **Critical Keys for Effective Praying.**

THE POWER OF PETITION:
Examining the Purpose of Prayer

"Prayer is not just about asking; it's about aligning our hearts with God's will, inviting His presence into our lives, and experiencing His transformative power."- Nicholas Robertson

Prayer stands as a vital element in the Christian journey, serving as our direct channel to commune with and honour the Lord. To comprehend its essence, we must dispel misconceptions. Prayer isn't about bargaining, making demands, or solely seeking favours. It's more than a therapeutic exercise or an attempt to control God; it's not a stage for displaying spirituality. Though petitioning God for needs is valid, prayer transcends mere requests. A. W. Tozer cautioned against reducing prayer to a mere wish-fulfilment mechanism, emphasising that God isn't a genie at our command. Jesus exemplified prayer in His earthly life. He prayed for Himself, others, and to commune with the Father. His prayer in John 17 epitomises this, not just seeking glory for the Father but also interceding for His disciples and future believers. He taught submission to God's will, evident in His prayer at Gethsemane.

Prayer also fortifies our bond with God. Like Jesus, individuals in relationship seek communication; prayer serves as our connection to God. Primarily, prayer is an act of worship—acknowledging God for His being and deeds. Many biblical instances portray prayer as worshipful reverence (e.g., 2 Kings 19:15, Psalm 86:12–13). Our prayers should reflect this focus on God rather than ourselves. The Lord's Prayer in Matthew 6:9–13 embodies these facets: it begins with adoration, then seeks God's will, includes petitions, and seeks strength against temptation. Jesus used this as a model, encapsulating prayer's diverse aspects with worship at its core. Warren Wiersbe encapsulates prayer's essence—fulfilling God's will on Earth and glorifying Him eternally. Prayer not only impacts lives but also fosters an intimate bond with God. Its significance is evident in Scripture, underscoring its unmissable place in the Christian walk.

Dear reader,
For more information on prayer, consider acquiring this book: **Critical Keys for Effective Praying.**

THE ART OF EFFECTIVE PRAYER:
Mastering the Language of the Heart

"Prayer becomes effective when our hearts align with God's will, our words reflect our trust in His sovereignty, and our actions demonstrate our faith in His promises."- Nicholas Robertson

In both the Old and New Testaments, God directs His people to pray. During crises, we easily petition the Lord for help, deliverance, provision, or healing, but there are times when we're unsure about what to pray for. Numerous prayer structures exist, like the five-finger prayer or the ACTS acronym. Jesus presents a model prayer in Matthew 6:10–13, providing ample prayer subjects:

"Our Father in heaven, may your name be honoured, may your kingdom come, may your will be done on earth as it is in heaven. Give us today our daily bread. And forgive us our sins, as we have forgiven those who sin against us. And don't let us yield to temptation but rescue us from the evil one."

This model serves as a framework for our personal prayers, a template adaptable to our requests. Let's explore each segment of Jesus' model to see how it applies to our prayer life:

"Our Father in heaven, may your name be honoured." We approach God solely, seeking to sanctify His name and reveal His holiness to the world.

"May your kingdom come; may your will be done on earth as it is in heaven." Before listing our needs, we align our desires with God's will, as Jesus exemplified in Gethsemane.

"Give us this day our daily bread." We're encouraged to ask for our daily necessities, including concerns troubling our hearts—be it job issues, family conflicts, financial strains, or soul-searching quests.

"Forgive us our sins, as we have forgiven those who sin against us." Seeking personal forgiveness can be painful, requiring sincere confession and a heart ready to forgive others.

"Don't let us yield to temptation but rescue us from the evil one." Acknowledging the presence of temptation, we implore God's protection and strength to overcome.

["For yours is the kingdom and the power and the glory forever. Amen."] Though not present in all manuscripts, it's beneficial. After making our requests, we reflect on God's greatness, submitting our will to His and acknowledging His worthiness of praise.

Though this model aids us, we're not confined to it. Prayer is continuous dialogue with God. As we grasp Scripture, we can incorporate it into our prayers, especially the Psalms that resonate with our situations. When unsure, we can turn to Psalms, echoing them back to their Author.

Dear reader,
For more information on prayer, consider acquiring this book: **Critical Keys for Effective Praying.**

THE SUBSTANCE OF HOPE:
Unravelling the Meaning of Faith

"Faith is the unwavering confidence in the unseen, the steadfast assurance that God's promises will be fulfilled, and the relentless trust in His love and providence."- Nicholas Robertson

Faith stands as the pinnacle of Christianity and the Christian journey. Though the Bible delves deeply into its essence, defining faith proves challenging. It surpasses mere belief in God's existence, evolving into a realm of trust. Authentic faith relinquishes all dependence on human effort, placing complete reliance on God's character, actions, and promises as revealed in His Word. Faith holds multifaceted dimensions; one being aptly described in Hebrews 11:1: "Now faith is confidence in what we hope for and assurance about what we do not see." It's about possessing presently unseen but hoped-for realities. God's Word, revealed truth, becomes our inner reality today, shifting our perspective from earthly to divine.

Paul affirms, "We walk by faith and not sight" (2 Corinthians 5:7). Faith isn't anchored in bank balances, news headlines, or medical reports. "We don't look at the troubles we can see now; rather, we fix our gaze on things that cannot be seen. For the things we see now will soon be gone, but the things we cannot see will last forever" (2 Corinthians 4:18, NLT). Amid a crumbling world, our faith remains secure in the unwavering promises of God and His Word.

Faith commences with God as a divine gift, not a human achievement. He initiates the relationship by revealing Himself and drawing individuals to Him (Ecclesiastes 3:11; Romans 1:19–20; 2 Peter 3:9; Isaiah 30:18), just as Jesus called His disciples (Matthew 4:18–22). God expects a response in faith, stating that it's impossible to please Him without it (Hebrews 11:6, NLT). Lack of trust in God underlined the first sin (Genesis 3:1–7). Since then, God persistently calls people back to faith—back to trust and obedience.

Faith has always been the sole means of salvation. In the Old Testament, the believer's expression of faith was through covenantal commitment. God initiated the covenant, and believers responded in faith, obeying His Word, and trusting in His promises. In Genesis 15:6, Abraham's faith was credited to him as righteousness (also, Romans 4:22; Galatians 3:6). The prophet asserts, "Look at the proud! They trust in themselves, but the righteous trust in God and live accordingly" (Habakkuk 2:4, NLT).

In the New Testament, faith is instrumental in receiving God's grace through Jesus Christ and the gift of salvation (Ephesians 2:8–9). Paul emphasises faith's centrality: "For I am not ashamed of this Good News about Christ. It is the power of God at work, saving everyone who believes—the Jew first and the Gentile. This Good News tells us how God makes us right in His sight. This is accomplished from start to finish by faith. As the Scriptures say, 'It is through faith that a righteous person has life'" (Romans 1:16–17, NLT; also, Romans 3:27–28; 10:9–10).

Faith yields countless blessings—salvation, justification, peace with God, indwelling of Christ in our hearts, forgiveness, adoption into God's family, divine protection and power, the freedom to draw near to God, reconciliation, sanctification, and new life in Jesus Christ. Moreover, it promises victory over death and eternal life.

The Bible teaches that faith isn't merely an attitude but is expressed through actions. James affirms that faith without actions is ineffectual (James 2:14, NLT). He doesn't advocate salvation by works but emphasises that faith and deeds are intertwined (James 2:26, NLT). Good works are evidence of living faith.

Biblical faith encompasses believing in God's existence and unwavering trust in His reliability. It prompts us to build our lives on Him and His Word, obeying its precepts regardless of what our physical eyes perceive. Through faith in Jesus Christ, we claim "the victory that has overcome the world" (1 John 5:4–5).

Dear reader,

Faith transcends mere belief and encompasses a deep conviction that God is faithful to His word and will fulfil His promises. Faith is not dependent on circumstances or visible evidence but is rooted in the character and nature of God. It empowers believers to persevere in the face of trials, to hope against hope, and to live with courage and conviction. As Hebrews 11:1 declares, "Now faith is the assurance of things hoped for, the conviction of things not seen." Faith is the lens through which we perceive the world and the driving force behind our relationship with God, guiding us in every aspect of our lives.

SURRENDERING TO SOVEREIGNTY:
Learning to Trust God Completely

"Trusting God is not about understanding His plan, but trusting His heart, knowing that He is always faithful, and His love never fails."- Nicholas Robertson

Understanding the concept of trust involves belief in the reliability, truth, and strength of a subject. Entrusting ourselves to God implies a deep-seated belief in His unwavering reliability, His unerring Word, His boundless ability, and His omnipotent strength. Scripture assures us of God's truthfulness, His steadfast commitment to promises, His boundless affection for us, and His benevolent intentions towards us. Trusting God means placing conviction in His divine statements about Himself, the world, and us.

It transcends mere sentiment; it's a deliberate choice to cling to His truth, even when feelings or circumstances beckon us towards doubt. Emotions and circumstances are significant and warrant attention, but relying solely on them for life's foundation is precarious. They're volatile, prone to abrupt shifts. Conversely, God remains constant – unchanging across time – rendering Him utterly dependable and deserving of our trust. Trusting God doesn't demand overlooking emotions or reality. It doesn't entail feigning contentment when life feels askew. Rather, it entails living a life deeply anchored in belief and adherence to God's ways, even amidst adversity.

Knowing what it entails to trust God, how do we actively incorporate this into our daily lives? In trusting relationships, openness thrives. God surpasses even the most reliable confidant; when life becomes arduous, He doesn't require us to hide our feelings.

"Cast all your anxiety on Him because He cares for you." (1 Peter 5:7, NIV) "You keep track of all my sorrows. You have collected all my tears in your bottle. You have recorded each one in Your book." (Psalm 56:8, NLT)

Given God's love for us, showcasing trust involves openly sharing every sentiment and circumstance – be it joy or trial – through prayer. Resist allowing emotions to govern; instead, bring them to God for His guiding hand. He's not dismayed or exasperated by our struggles, uncertainties, or anguish. He genuinely cares, and in Him, we can confide our deepest concerns.

In moments of adversity, trusting entails seeking solace in God's Word and acting obediently, trusting Him to navigate the rest. It doesn't seek assurance in worldly facets but finds security in God amidst trying times. We won't do this perfectly, but God patiently guides us along this path. Even Jesus felt overwhelmed, yet He turned to His Father. God attends to your hurts, paying meticulous attention. How reassuring it is to realise that the Creator of the universe is attuned to your needs. Knowing that God is on your side fortifies your trust amidst hardships and the unknown.

Trust flourishes when we truly comprehend the object of our trust. When someone says, "Trust me," our reaction tends to be either compliance or scepticism. Trust in God naturally ensues when we grasp why we should trust Him.

Foremost, God is inherently deserving of our trust. Unlike humans, He never lies or falters in fulfilling promises. "God is not a man, that He should lie, nor a son of man, that He should change His mind. Does He speak and then not act? Does He promise and not fulfil?" (Numbers 23:19; Psalm 89:34). He possesses the omnipotence to realise His plans flawlessly, remaining steadfast in His flawless, righteous designs. Moreover, He orchestrates everything for good for those who love Him (Romans 8:28). Understanding these attributes through His Word compels us to place our unwavering trust in Him.

We learn to trust God by witnessing His unwavering faithfulness in our lives and in history. Records in 1 Kings 8:56 affirm God's fidelity in fulfilling promises, reflected both in His Word and through personal experiences. Christians can testify to His trustworthiness as He saves souls, shapes lives for His divine purpose, and provides solace amidst life's complexities. Experiencing His grace and constancy amplifies our trust (Psalm 100:5; Isaiah 25:1).

Finally, when pondering trust, we encounter a logical choice. Should we entrust ourselves to fallible, unpredictable humans or the all-knowing, all-powerful, loving God? Embracing God's trustworthiness becomes an inherent part of our journey as we get to know Him through His Word. Understanding breed's trust.

Dear reader,
For more information on faith, consider acquiring my book: **Positive Vibration: Biblical Keys for Faith Activation.**

THE SACRED SCRIPTURES:
Examining the Bible

"The Bible is not just a book; it is a living, breathing testament to God's love, wisdom, and faithfulness, offering guidance, comfort, and hope to all who seek its truths."- Nicholas Robertson

The word "Bible" originates from Latin and Greek, meaning "book," fitting for a timeless book meant for all people. This exceptional book stands alone, composed of sixty-six distinct books spanning various genres: law, history, poetry, prophecy, narratives, proverbs, parables, biographies, and epistles.

About 40 human authors contributed to this extraordinary book over approximately 1500 years. The writers hailed from diverse backgrounds—kings, fishermen, priests, officials, farmers, shepherds, and physicians. Yet, from this diversity emerges a remarkable unity, with consistent themes interwoven throughout.

The Bible's unity stems from having one ultimate Author—God Himself. It's described as "God-breathed" (2 Timothy 3:16), where human authors inscribed precisely what God intended, resulting in the flawless and sacred Word of God (Psalm 12:6; 2 Peter 1:21).

The Bible divides into two primary sections: the Old Testament and the New Testament. In essence, the Old Testament narrates the story of a nation, while the New Testament tells of a Man. The nation, Israel, paved the way for the arrival of Jesus Christ. The Old Testament unfolds the establishment and preservation of Israel as a nation. God pledged to use Israel as a blessing to the entire world (Genesis 12:2-3). Within this nation, God elevated the family of David, from which one Man was prophesied to bring the promised blessing (Isaiah 11:1-10).

The New Testament chronicles the arrival of that promised Man, Jesus. He fulfilled Old Testament prophecies, leading a flawless life, sacrificing Himself as the Saviour, and triumphantly rising from death. Jesus is the central figure of the Bible—its entire narrative revolves around Him. The Old Testament anticipates His arrival, while the New Testament reveals His work to deliver salvation to our sinful world. Jesus transcends being merely a historical figure or even a human; He's God incarnate, embodying the clearest, most comprehensible depiction of God. Wondering what God is like? Look to Jesus—He embodies God in human form (John 1:14, 14:9).

The Bible encompasses God's creation of man in a perfect setting, man's rebellion leading to his fall, and God's response—placing the world under a curse while setting in motion a plan to restore humanity and creation to its original glory.

This redemption plan includes God calling Abraham out of Babylonia to Canaan around 2000 B.C., promising to bless the world through his descendants. Israel, originating from Abraham, migrated to Egypt, grew into a nation, and was later led out by Moses around 1400 B.C. to their promised land, Canaan. God established a covenant with them through Moses and conveyed the Law.

Fast forward—God's promise to David and Solomon for an everlasting king from their lineage, Israel's division, and subsequent downfall due to idolatry, Babylon's captivity, the gracious return of a remnant to rebuild Jerusalem, and the close of the Old Testament.

The New Testament begins about 400 years later, documenting Jesus Christ's birth in Bethlehem, fulfilling God's plan for redemption. Jesus, fulfilling His role, died for sins, rose from death, establishing a new covenant. His disciples spread this message globally, with the New

Testament concluding with the anticipation of Jesus' return to judge the world and restore creation.

Dear reader,

For more information on the Bible and How to interpret it, consider acquiring these books: **Critical Keys for Biblical Interpretation 1 and 2.**

THE VERACITY OF SCRIPTURE:
Exploring the Foundation of Belief in the Bible

"The Bible is not only trustworthy because it claims to be the Word of God; it is trustworthy because throughout history, its truths have transformed lives, imparted wisdom, and provided hope to countless generations."- Nicholas Robertson

The Bible encompasses claims about the universe's creation, the character of its divine Creator who reigns supreme, and the destiny of humanity. If these assertions hold true, the Bible becomes the most crucial book in human history. Its truthfulness potentially unravels life's grandest queries: "Where do I come from?" "Why do I exist?" and "What occurs after death?" The Bible's significance warrants fair consideration, and its message's veracity is observable, testable, and capable of enduring scrutiny.

According to the Bible's writers, the Scriptures represent God's very utterances. The apostle Paul asserts that "all Scripture is God-breathed" (2 Timothy 3:16), implying that the original writings stemmed from God's mouth before reaching the pens of its human authors. Similarly, the apostle Peter notes that prophecy never originated from human will but was spoken by individuals carried along by the Holy Spirit (2 Peter 1:21). The phrase "carried along" indicates a sail driven by the wind, elucidating the influence of the Holy Spirit in scripting the Bible. As a result, the Bible doesn't have its roots in humanity but instead emanates from God, thus holding divine authority.

However, it's critical to avoid circular reasoning as the justification for believing in the Bible. Relying on the Bible's self-attestation to believe in itself isn't sufficient. Yet, if its truth claims withstand scrutiny and align with historical and scientific discoveries, the Bible's internal claims about its trustworthiness gain substantial credibility, reinforced by external evidence.

The internal evidence for Scripture's authenticity presents compelling arguments for its believability. Its unique message stands apart from other religious texts, painting a stark picture of humanity's inherent sinfulness and incapacity to rectify this state, contrary to human inclinations to portray themselves favourably.

Moreover, the Bible's unity across a span of roughly 1,550 years, involving diverse human authors from varying backgrounds, environments, and languages, crafting a coherent message from Genesis to Revelation, defies the odds of fallibility. Its consistency is striking despite covering contentious subjects.

Another reason bolstering belief in the Bible is its accuracy. While not a science textbook, the Bible addresses scientific themes; it foretold the water cycle long before its scientific discovery. At times, apparent conflicts between science and the Bible have arisen, yet as science progresses, biblical accuracy stands firm. For instance, the Bible's stance on the importance of blood, aligning with modern medical understanding, contrasts historical practices like excessive bloodletting.

The Bible's accuracy extends to its historical truth claims. Scepticism about biblical references like the Hittite people was dispelled by archaeological discoveries, confirming the Bible's accounts.

Furthermore, the Bible contains fulfilled prophecies made by its writers' centuries in advance, showcasing its supernatural accuracy. The fulfilment of numerous prophecies, especially about Jesus, reinforces the credibility of Scripture.

In every test, the Bible's truthfulness holds, encompassing spiritual truths as well. Whether affirming historical events or detailing spiritual realities like humanity's sinful nature and God's redemptive plan through Jesus Christ, the Bible stands as a testament to its reliability.

Dear reader,
For more information on the Bible and How to interpret it, consider acquiring these books: **Critical Keys for Biblical Interpretation 1 and 2.**

ILLUMINATING TRUTH:
Exploring the Purpose of the Bible

"The Bible's purpose is not merely to provide answers, but to lead us into a deeper relationship with God, to reveal His character, His will, and His unending love for humanity."- Nicholas Robertson

The Bible stands as both extraordinary literature and the ultimate best-seller of all time. Within its pages lie history, captivating tales, poetry, philosophy, and personal letters. However, its primary significance transcends these—it's God's Word. Its single most critical purpose is to unveil God to us. It reveals facets about God that we could never discern unless He communicated them. Moreover, the Bible informs us about ourselves, delineating our sin and God's redemptive plan through Jesus Christ.

Second Timothy 3:15–17 provides a comprehensive insight into the Bible's purpose. Paul instructs Timothy that the Scriptures, from childhood, were instrumental in making him wise for salvation through faith in Christ Jesus. Every portion of the Bible is "God-breathed," beneficial for teaching, correcting, rebuking, and training in righteousness, thoroughly equipping God's servant for good works. Whether spoken directly by God or guided by Him through men, all of it is His authoritative Word, guiding us towards salvation and righteousness.

Numerous verses in the Bible further expound on its purposes in our lives:

- It steers us away from sin: "How can a young person stay on the path of purity? By living according to your word" (Psalm 119:9).
- It provides spiritual guidance: "Your word is a lamp for my feet, a light on my path" (Psalm 119:105).
- Some sections aim to give an accurate account of Jesus for our belief in Him and eternal life: "But these are written that you may believe that Jesus is the Messiah, the Son of God, and that by believing you may have life in his name" (John 20:30–31).
- It assures believers of their salvation: "I write these things to you who believe in the name of the Son of God so that you may know that you have eternal life" (1 John 5:13).
- The psalmist David exults in the Word of God and its purpose in his life, recognising its perfection, trustworthiness, and transformative power (Psalm 19:7–11).
- When tempted by Satan, Jesus countered by asserting the supremacy of God's Word over physical sustenance,

showcasing its essentiality and the means to resist temptation (Matthew 4:4).

- The Bible helps us grasp our true selves and navigate through the distractions of popular culture that may lead us astray from God's path. Its living and active nature penetrates deeply, discerning the thoughts and attitudes of our hearts (Hebrews 4:12).
- The Bible's impact surpasses human cleverness or efforts; it carries the transformative power of God's Word when proclaimed faithfully (Isaiah 55:10–11).

However, the Bible isn't a mere collection of aphorisms; it's a cohesive work that must be diligently studied in context. Christians seeking to honour God should regularly consume God's Word. Similarly, sceptics or the curious should engage with the Bible firsthand to explore its essence.

Dear reader,

For more information on the Bible and How to interpret it, consider acquiring these books: **Critical Keys for Biblical Interpretation 1 and 2.**

HEARTFELT DEVOTION:
Understanding the Meaning of Worship

"Worship is not just an event; it's a lifestyle—a continual expression of love, adoration, and surrender to the One who is worthy of all praise."- Nicholas Robertson

The apostle Paul's profound words in Romans 12:1-2 encapsulate the core of genuine worship. This passage outlines the motivating factors, and the way true worship is expressed. It begins with the compelling motivation behind worship: God's abundant mercies. These mercies encompass an array of gifts bestowed upon us by God, stirring within us a deep sense of gratitude and adoration—essentially, the foundation of worship itself.

The manner of our worship is detailed as offering ourselves—our entire beings—as living, holy sacrifices unto God. This sacrifice extends beyond mere physical actions; it encompasses surrendering our hearts, minds, thoughts, and attitudes, symbolising complete submission to God's will. However, this submission is achieved through the renewal of our minds—a continuous process involving cleansing our thoughts of worldly influences and embracing the wisdom found in God's truth.

The pivotal role of God's Word emerges as the primary agent in renewing our minds. It unveils the truth about God's mercies and fosters a profound affection and conviction that naturally inspires true spiritual worship. Worship, then, is not rooted in external stimuli, such as music, but emanates from a heart captivated by God's mercies and obedient to His teachings.

Crucially, authentic worship is centred on God, not on external rituals, music, or public perception. It's about worshiping God with our whole being, guided by truth and a heartfelt connection with Him. This worship can manifest through various acts—prayer, reading Scripture, singing, partaking in communion, or serving others—always stemming from a heart in alignment with God's design.

A key aspect of genuine worship is its exclusivity for God alone. Worshipping saints, idols, or expecting personal gain contradicts the essence of true worship. Worship should be sincere, devoid of hypocrisy or obligation, seeking solely to honour and please God. Scripture emphasises that authentic worship extends beyond church gatherings, as it encompasses every aspect of life—honouring God through obedience, knowledge of Him, and glorification of His power and glory.

Dear reader,

Genuine worship goes beyond rituals or outward expressions; it's about acknowledging God's supremacy and demonstrating loyalty and admiration toward Him. It's a heartfelt response to His mercy, a constant surrender of ourselves to His will, and an acknowledgment of His greatness in everything we do. True worship is the reverent acknowledgment of God's majesty and the heartfelt praise expressed through a life devoted to His Word and obedience.

THE HEART OF WORSHIP:
Exploring the Heart of True Devotion

"Worship is not about performance or presentation; it's about the posture of our hearts, the surrender of our wills, and the adoration of our Creator."- Nicholas Robertson

In the heart of worship, beyond the confines of religious rituals or traditional expressions, lies an essence that transcends mere actions—a sincere devotion to God. It begins with Joshua's resolute declaration: "As for me and my house, we will serve the Lord," epitomising a family's committed dedication to divine service.

Service to the Lord is rooted in understanding the depth of worship. Originating from the Greek word "Proskuneo," worship embodies a gesture akin to a respectful kiss—an act of reverence and devotion. This reverence is further emphasised in the Hebrew term "Shachah," signifying the act of bowing down, a posture of humble adoration before God's presence.

However, true worship extends far beyond superficial acts. It's not confined to the slow melodies of choirs or the offering baskets. Worship isn't limited to outward expressions or church attendance. It's a deeply intimate connection, an extravagant love, and an extreme submission to God—a lifestyle marked by holiness and devotion.

Distinct from praise, which can be expressed by anyone, worship emanates from a sober realisation of God's identity. It's not merely acknowledging God's blessings but honouring Him for His inherent worthiness. Ascribing glory and strength to His name isn't an obligation but an authentic expression of profound love and submission.

True worship centres on the priority of God in our lives. It's not contingent on evident miraculous signs or blessings but on recognising God's sovereignty and inherent worthiness. It isn't about what God can do for us but acknowledging who He is—the omnipotent, omniscient, and omnipresent One.

Why do we worship? The reason lies in acknowledging God's intrinsic worthiness, not merely His deeds. Our worship isn't merely a response to blessings received; it's an authentic expression of adoration for who God is—an Omnipotent Creator deserving of reverence.

Dear reader,

Worship is a devotion reserved for God alone, not contingent on external circumstances or blessings. It's a heartfelt acknowledgment of God's worthiness, an expression of love, and an unwavering commitment, irrespective of life's situations.

EXALTING THE ALMIGHTY:
Understanding the Meaning of Praise

"Praising God is not just about lifting our voices in song; it's about lifting our hearts in gratitude, awe, and reverence for His goodness, His greatness, and His grace."- Nicholas Robertson

Christians often emphasise the act of "praising God," a command echoed throughout the Bible for all living beings to lift their voices in worship (Psalm 150:6). In the embroidery of spiritual expression, one of the most vibrant threads is praise. It's not merely an act but a symphony of the soul—a way of honouring and magnifying God. Praise transcends the limits of language, offering a melodic tribute to the Creator. At its core, praise embodies a multifaceted essence, woven through the scriptures and diverse cultures. The Hebrew language captures its hues through various words, each painting a different stroke of this profound expression. In Hebrew, various words capture the essence of praise. "Yadah" encapsulates praise, thanksgiving, and confession. Another term, "zamar," translates to "sing praise," while "halal," the root of "hallelujah," signifies honouring and commending. Each term embodies gratitude and homage toward the worthy subject of praise.

The Psalms, a treasury of songs, resound with praises directed to God. Psalm 9 joyfully expresses, "I will be glad and rejoice in you; I will sing the praises of your name, O Most High" (Psalm 9:2). Psalm 18:3 reveres God as "worthy of praise," while Psalm 21:13 exalts His divine attributes and mighty power.

Psalm 150 resounds with the word "praise" thirteen times in six verses. The first verse sets the scene for praise—everywhere! "Praise God in His sanctuary; praise Him in His mighty heavens."

The subsequent verse illuminates the reason behind praising the Lord: "Praise Him for His acts of power; praise Him for His surpassing greatness." Verses 3–6 outline the manner of praising the Lord—utilising various instruments, dance, and the breath of every living being. Every means to produce sound is to be employed in praising the Lord!

The New Testament carries forward this grand melody of praise. It recounts instances where Jesus, the epitome of divine embodiment, received homage and adoration from those who recognised His glory and authority.

Matthew 21:16 echoes the praise offered to Jesus as He entered Jerusalem, celebrated as the triumphant King.

Matthew 8:2 depicts the humble acknowledgment of His authority, as a leper bows in reverence before the Son of God.

Matthew 28:17 witnesses the disciples worshiping Jesus after His resurrection, acknowledging His divinity.

The early Christian communities actively engaged in collective worship. The inaugural church in Jerusalem held worship as a focal point (Acts 2:42–43). In Antioch, church leaders prayed, worshiped, and fasted as they commissioned Paul and Barnabas for missionary work (Acts 13:1–5). Many of Paul's epistles feature extensive sections praising the Lord (1 Timothy 3:14–16; Philippians 1:3–11).

Praise, a masterpiece of adoration, lifts the soul into the divine presence, surpassing earthly bounds. It's more than commendation; it's an expression of worship, glorifying and honouring the Almighty. Within its embrace, we find ourselves humbled, our attention centred upon the Lord, pouring out heartfelt love, adoration, and gratitude. Authentic praise propels us into divine fellowship, heightening our awareness of spiritual union with God. It acts as a bridge to the supernatural, a conduit to His boundless power. Psalms resound with exultant praise, ushering believers into intimacy with the Most High. Praise isn't reserved for the sanctuary; it's a constant in the life of a believer. It permeates daily existence, infusing every moment with the refreshing presence and anointing of the Lord. It's a declaration of faith, a sacrificial offering to God, not governed by feelings but by a deep-seated belief in His sovereignty and desire to please Him. "Therefore, by Him let us continually offer the sacrifice of praise to God, that is, the fruit of our lips, giving thanks to His name" (Hebrews 13:15). Praise becomes a weapon against spiritual adversaries. A humble, worship-filled atmosphere repels darkness, terrifying the enemy. As seen in Chronicles, the power of praise routed hostile forces and proclaimed victory.

"...when they began to sing and to praise, the LORD set ambushes against the people of Ammon, Moab, and Mount Seir, who had come against Judah; and they were defeated" (2 Chronicles 20:22).

Paul and Silas midnight hymns in prison highlight a intense truth: true praise unlocks divine presence and power. Their worshipful hearts created an atmosphere where God's miraculous intervention was inevitable. Acts 16:23-26 "And when they had laid many stripes on them, they threw them into prison, commanding the jailer to keep them securely.

Having received such a charge, he put them into the inner prison and fastened their feet in the stocks. But at midnight Paul and Silas were praying and singing hymns to God, and the prisoners were listening to them. Suddenly there was a great earthquake, so that the foundations of the prison were shaken, and immediately all the doors swung open.

Praise is not a mere reaction to God's presence; it's a vehicle to access His glory. It invites God to dwell among worshippers, infusing gatherings with His divine presence.

Worship is not a response to the Holy Spirit's movement; it catalyses His manifestation. Lifting up Christ through worship invites His anointing and power to permeate our midst. Praise isn't just an act; it's the resonating song of the heart, a tribute of gratitude, and a harmonious chorus celebrating El Shadai. Its quintessence, interwoven with various words, melodies, and gestures, invites every soul to partake in the concord of worship. In praise, we discover a key to unlocking the channel to God's presence and power. It goes beyond the mundane, ushering us into a realm where the celestial and terrestrial converge. Embrace the work of praise; it's more than a song—it's a gateway to the miraculous.

Dear reader,

In the culmination of time, God's people will unite in eternal praise. "No longer will there be anything accursed, but the throne of God and of the Lamb will be in it, and His servants will worship Him" (Revelation 22:3). Freed from sin's curse, the faithful will forever extol the King of kings in an unblemished state. It is said that our earthly worship serves as a preparatory rehearsal for the grand celebration of eternal praise alongside the Lord.

GRATITUDE IN ACTION:
Exploring the Meaning of Thankfulness

"Thankfulness is not just an attitude; it's a lifestyle—a continual recognition of God's goodness, a constant acknowledgment of His blessings, and a perpetual posture of gratitude."- Nicholas Robertson

Gratitude is a recurring theme throughout the Bible, urging believers to embrace a spirit of thankfulness in all situations. The Scriptures in 1 Thessalonians 5:16-18 emphasise the call to rejoice, pray continually, and give thanks regardless of circumstances. This concept of gratitude is foundational, seamlessly emerging from the depths of our hearts and echoing through our words and actions. Delving deeper into Scripture unveils not just the why but also the how of maintaining an attitude of gratitude in various life scenarios. Psalm 136:1 underscores the thoughtful reasons for thanksgiving—God's enduring goodness and unfailing love. Gratitude wells up within us as we recognise our inherent brokenness and acknowledge that apart from God, there is only despair and death. Acknowledging God's constant goodness and steadfast love becomes the catalyst for our gratitude.

Consider Psalm 30, where David extols God for deliverance from distressing circumstances. In the midst of adversity, David's praise for God's deliverance isn't just a response to a specific moment but a reflection on God's consistent faithfulness in the past. It's a celebration of God's character, inspiring sincere praise as the only suitable response.

Psalm 28 mirrors David's distress, a heartfelt plea for mercy, protection, and justice. Even amidst turmoil, David acknowledges God's sovereignty and expresses gratitude, drawing strength and comfort from trusting God.

Instances in the New Testament, such as Paul's persecution, reveal a similar spirit of thanksgiving. Despite hardships, Paul gives thanks to God, recognising His triumphant guidance. The writers of Hebrews and Peter echo the sentiment of thanksgiving in the face of trials, accentuating that hardships refine faith and lead to eternal honour and glory.

The kernel of gratitude stems from a deep awareness of God's immeasurable blessings. The Scriptures warn of an absence of thanksgiving in the last days, highlighting its significance in a believer's life. Expressing gratitude directs our focus away from self-centred desires or current struggles, reminding us of God's ultimate sovereignty and the multitude of spiritual blessings bestowed upon us.

Dear reader,

Thanksgiving isn't merely appropriate but strongly beneficial. It surpasses personal benefits, grounding us in the truth that we belong to God and are blessed with spiritual riches. Ultimately, gratitude is a testament to the abundant life we've received, making it a fitting response to God's goodness.

UNDERSTANDING SEXUAL PURITY:
Exploring the Concept of Sexual Immorality

"Sexual immorality is not just a physical act; it's a betrayal of trust, a violation of intimacy, and a distortion of God's design for love and relationships."

Within the New Testament, the term frequently rendered as "sexual immorality" is "porneia." Translated variously as "whoredom," "fornication," and "idolatry," it signifies a forfeiture of sexual purity and typically references premarital relations. From this Greek term emerges "pornography," aligning with the concept of "selling off." Sexual immorality equates to the relinquishing of purity and encompasses any sexual expression outside the framework of biblically defined marital unions (Matthew 19:4–5). The link between sexual immorality and idolatry finds context in 1 Corinthians 6:18: "Flee from sexual immorality. All other sins a person commits are outside the body, but he who sins sexually sins against his own body." The bodies of believers serve as the "temple of the Holy Spirit" (1 Corinthians 6:19–20). Pagan idol worship often intertwined with perverse and immoral sexual practices within the precincts of false deities' temples.

Engaging in immoral actions with our bodies echoes pagan rituals, desecrating God's sacred dwelling with detestable acts (1 Corinthians 6:9–11).

The Biblical proscriptions against sexual immorality frequently align with warnings against "impurity" (Romans 1:24; Galatians 5:19; Ephesians 4:19). The Greek term "akatharsia" signifies "defiled, foul, ceremonially unfit." Such actions render an individual unfit for God's presence. Continuous indulgence in unrepentant immorality and impurity precludes communion with God. Jesus affirmed, "Blessed are the pure in heart, for they shall see God" (Matthew 5:8; cf. Psalm 24:3–4). Sustaining a healthy bond with God remains impossible if our bodies and souls are steeped in impurity.

Sexuality, a design of God, falls under His jurisdiction for regulation. The Bible unambiguously stipulates that sexual relations were intended for enjoyment between one man and one woman within a lifelong covenant of marriage until death separates them (Matthew 19:6). Sexuality represents God's sacred gift to humanity, and any deviation from these parameters constitutes an abuse of this divine endowment. Adultery, premarital sex, pornography, and homosexual relationships all contravene God's design and thus fall under the category of sin. Several objections are commonly raised against God's directives on sexual immorality:

"It's not wrong if we love each other." The Bible does not differentiate between "loving" and "unloving" sexual relationships; it distinguishes between married and unmarried individuals. Sex within marriage is blessed (Genesis 1:28), while sex outside of marriage is termed "fornication" or "sexual immorality" (1 Corinthians 7:2–5).

"Times have changed, and biblical sins no longer apply." Most passages denouncing sexual immorality also encompass evils like greed, lust, stealing, etc. (1 Corinthians 6:9–10; Galatians 5:19–21). We acknowledge these as persistent sins. God's character remains constant, unaffected by cultural shifts (Malachi 3:6; Numbers 23:19; Hebrews 13:8).

"We're married in God's eyes." This notion overlooks God's unchanging commands. Marriage, as ordained by God, involves one man and one woman bound for life (Mark 10:6–9). The Bible often uses the imagery of weddings and covenant marriages as metaphors for imparting spiritual truths (Matthew 22:2; Revelation 19:9). God takes marriage seriously and perceives immorality regardless of how skilfully we redefine it.

"I can maintain a good relationship with God despite my actions." Proverbs 28:9 asserts, "If one turns away his ear from hearing the law, even his prayer is an abomination."

Holding onto sin while presuming God's indifference is self-deception. First John 2:3–4 challenges those adopting this line of thinking: "We know that we have come to know Him if we keep His commands. Whoever says, 'I know Him,' but does not do what He commands is a liar, and the truth is not in that person."

Hebrews 13:4 clarifies God's expectations for His children: "Let marriage be held in honour among all, and let the marriage bed be undefiled, for God will judge the sexually immoral and adulterous." Sexual immorality is unequivocally wrong. Through repentance and acceptance of Jesus' forgiveness (1 John 1:7–9), our old nature and its practices, including sexual immorality, must be extinguished (Romans 6:12–14; 8:13). Ephesians 5:3 cautions against even a hint of sexual immorality, impurity, or greed, for they are improper for God's holy people.

Dear reader,

For more on sexual purity, consider acquiring my books: **Before You Say I Do: 21 Considerations to Ponder Before Constructing a Thriving Marriage and After You Say I Do: 21 Considerations for Constructing a Thriving Marriage.**

GUARDING THE HEART:
Understanding the Importance of Sexual Purity

"Sexual purity matters because it honours God's design for intimacy, preserves the sanctity of relationships, and protects the heart from the scars of betrayal and brokenness."- Nicholas Robertson

For aeons, the discourse on sex and the Biblical restrictions surrounding it has engendered debate, discord, and disregard. "Why does God concern Himself with my intimate relationships? Why does sexual conduct merit such scrutiny? Aren't there more pressing matters than my personal life?" There's a murmuring chorus that suggests Christians magnify the Bible's sexual constraints disproportionately. The muttering often echoes: "Why is it that sex, a mere fraction of the Ten Commandments, garners so much emphasis?" (Though in fairness, two commandments—adultery and coveting a neighbour's spouse—address it, but that's a tangent.)

Two vital points emerge from this maelstrom of thoughts:
- Why is divine interest piqued in our choice of partners?
- Does Christianity's stern stance against extramarital relations hold merit?

Unequivocally, who we sleep with matters to God. In the records of scripture, 1 Corinthians 6:18 issues a clear directive: "Flee from sexual immorality. Every other sin a person commits is outside the body, but the sexually immoral person sins against his own body." Though contextually addressing prostitution in Corinth, Paul's exhortation transcends those limits. His stance: sexual sin inflicts a unique, profound harm upon oneself. Drawing from Genesis 2:24 in 1 Corinthians 6:16, Paul reinforces the concept of becoming one flesh through sex—an intimate union that extends beyond the physical. Sex, Paul contends, transcends mere physicality; it's a binding of spirits, emotions, and bodies. To argue that sex is "just sex" finds no foothold in the Bible. It's a transformative act, never devoid of consequence. Having intercourse offers a piece of oneself, a loving union celebrated within marriage but hazardous outside it. Despite attempts to disengage emotions or render it inconsequential, sex leaves an indelible mark. If the Bible warns strenuously against it, there must be consequences, even if unspecified. God's interest in our sexual conduct stems from a desire for us to experience it at its zenith. His guidelines aren't intended to deprive but to enhance the depth, intimacy, and unity inherent in this act.

The Bible reinforces God's stance against extramarital sexual relations, and we should too. Reflecting on my teen years as a Christian, I recall the repetition of "no sex before marriage" and my impatience for a broader discourse. Presently, as an adult, I grasp the significance. As Paul notes, sexual immorality is self-destructive. Christianity emphasises this topic because society largely embraces sexual sin. Unlike theft or murder, where consensus on wrongdoing persists, the world opposes the Bible's stance on premarital sex, adultery, and homosexuality. Ergo, Christian's vocalise on sexual immorality more fervently. Imagine a world celebrating theft; Christians would ardently oppose it, promoting Biblical teachings against stealing. They'd disseminate messages from Exodus 20:15, fashion gloves bearing anti-theft slogans, and hold seminars for kleptomaniacs. Sexual discourse takes centre stage for its gravity. It's an issue where Christianity and the world diverge. Consider, too, the tangible fallout: STDs, unplanned pregnancies, ruptured marriages, and fractured families—all potential outcomes of flouting Biblical guidelines. Complying with God's directives reaps numerous benefits and safeguards against adverse consequences. God's concern about our sexual partners doesn't stem from a tyrannical disposition. It springs from His desire for our well-being. The Christian stand against extramarital sex is warranted, but our communication could be more comprehensive and compassionate. Truth should be accompanied by love, adhering to Ephesians 4:15. Yet, allowing self-inflicted harm without a cautionary voice contradicts love's essence.

Dear reader,

For more information on sexual purity, consider acquiring my books: **Before You Say I Do: 21 Considerations to Ponder Before Constructing a Thriving Marriage, After You Say I Do: 21 Considerations for Constructing a Thriving Marriage.**

THE TEMPTATION OF LUST:
Understanding Its Nature and Consequences

"Lust is the counterfeit of love, enticing with promises of pleasure but ultimately leaving the soul impoverished and unfulfilled."

The concept of lust is defined as an intense desire for something or someone, often specifically linked with sexual desires. Lust primarily centres around self-fulfilment, often disregarding the potential adverse consequences. Greed is closely entwined with the idea of lust. Various desires, especially those of selfish nature, are specifically addressed within the Ten Commandments, prohibiting coveting a neighbour's property or possessions (Exodus 20:14-17).

Regarding sexual lust, Jesus, in His Sermon on the Mount, addressed this issue by delving into the heart of the matter. Contrary to prevailing Jewish teachings that considered only the act of adultery as sinful, Jesus emphasised a deeper truth: "You have heard that it was said, 'You shall not commit adultery.' But I say to you that everyone who looks at a woman with lustful intent has already committed adultery with her in his heart" (Matthew 5:27-28). Lust constitutes a sin both in thought and action, challenging the cultural notion that "looking is fine if you don't touch."

Lust, whether sexual or otherwise, is a grave sin before God: "But each person is tempted when he is lured and enticed by his own desire. Then desire when it has conceived gives birth to sin, and sin when it is fully grown brings forth death" (James 1:14-15). It's a pathway that leads to sin and eventual destruction.

How can a believer confront the issue of lust?

Two biblical approaches are particularly relevant. Firstly, Jesus advised eliminating the triggers or pathways leading to specific lustful temptations. He employed an exaggerated illustration to stress this point: "If your right eye causes you to sin, tear it out and throw it away… And if your right hand causes you to sin, cut it off and throw it away" (Matthew 5:29-30).

Obviously, this doesn't advocate literal self-mutilation but underscores the necessity to remove the stimuli triggering lust. For some, this might mean installing internet filters to block access to pornography, while for others, it could involve avoiding specific films or places in town.

Secondly, seeking contentment as taught in the Bible can counteract lustful desires. The apostle Paul wrote about this:

"I have learned in whatever situation I am to be content... I can do all things through Him who strengthens me" (Philippians 4:11-13). Complete reliance on Christ and spiritual growth can replace and alleviate the hold of lust.

Dear reader,

Lust and temptation are perennial struggles faced by individuals striving for moral integrity and spiritual purity. Lust, often fuelled by fleeting desires and worldly attractions, can lead individuals astray from their values and commitments. It arises from a fixation on physical gratification and a disregard for the sacredness of human relationships. Temptation, on the other hand, is the insidious lure that seeks to entice individuals into compromising their principles and succumbing to sinful desires. It presents itself in various forms, exploiting vulnerabilities and testing one's resolved to resist. Both lust and temptation challenge individuals to exercise self-control, cultivate spiritual discipline, and rely on the strength of their faith to overcome. By recognizing the destructive nature of lust and the subtle allure of temptation, individuals can guard their hearts and minds, seeking refuge in prayer, scripture, and the support of a supportive community. Through vigilance and reliance on God's grace, they can navigate the treacherous waters of lust and temptation, emerging stronger and more resilient in their journey towards spiritual maturity.

EXPLORING ROMANTIC CONNECTIONS:
Exploring the Dynamics of Dating

"Dating is not just about finding someone to spend time with; it's about discovering compatibility, building trust, and discerning whether two hearts are meant to journey together."- Nicholas Robertson

The terms "courtship" and "dating" don't specifically appear in the Bible, but it does offer principles for how Christians should navigate relationships before marriage. One crucial principle is to distance ourselves from the world's dating standards since they often contradict God's ways (2 Peter 2:20). Instead of the world's approach of dating casually, it's vital to understand a person's character before committing. Seeking if someone has been reborn in the Spirit of Christ (John 3:3-8) and shares a pursuit of Christ-like qualities (Philippians 2:5) is essential. The end goal of dating or courtship is discovering a life partner. Scripture warns against marrying an unbeliever (2 Corinthians 6:14-15) as it can weaken our bond with Christ and compromise our values.

In committed relationships, whether dating or courting, prioritising love for the Lord above all else is essential

(Matthew 10:37). Elevating someone to the status of being "everything" in life amounts to idolatry and sinful (Galatians 5:20; Colossians 3:5). Upholding purity and abstaining from premarital sex is emphasised (1 Corinthians 6:9, 13; 2 Timothy 2:22). Sexual immorality not only offends God but also defiles our bodies (1 Corinthians 6:18). Honouring and loving others as we love ourselves (Romans 12:9-10) applies strongly to dating or courting relationships. Adhering to these biblical principles forms a secure foundation for marriage, one of life's most critical decisions. Marriage unites two individuals into an unbreakable bond intended by God to be permanent (Genesis 2:24; Matthew 19:5).

Dating and courtship represent two distinct approaches to initiating relationships with the opposite sex. While some non-Christians view dating as a path to physical intimacy, for Christians, such motivations are unacceptable. Many see dating as a stage of friendship, preserving this aspect until both individuals are ready to consider commitment as potential marriage partners. Central to dating for Christians is discovering if their potential partner shares their faith in Christ, following the biblical injunction against marriages between believers and unbelievers (2 Corinthians 6:14–15). Christian believers dating is advised to maintain limited physical contact to avoid temptation (1 Corinthians 6:18–20). Advocates of courtship propose an even stricter approach, advocating for no physical contact until marriage—no touching, handholding, or kissing. In courtship, couples often involve family members, especially parents, in their interactions and clarify their intentions upfront—to explore compatibility for marriage. Proponents argue that courtship allows individuals to get to know each other in a platonic setting, devoid of the pressures of physical intimacy or emotional entanglements. Both dating and courtship come with inherent challenges. For daters, spending time alone with someone attractive of the opposite sex can present tempting situations. Setting clear boundaries is essential, ensuring that Christ is honoured in their interactions. In courtship, while some find it an ideal way to find a life partner, others see it as oppressive and controlling. The lack of one-on-one time might obscure the true essence of a person, and some courtship scenarios can feel akin to arranged marriages, leading to resentment. Neither dating nor courtship is mandated in Scripture. Ultimately, the couple's Christian character and spiritual maturity are more significant than the specifics of how they spend time together. The goal, regardless of the method used, should be godly individuals forming families that honour God. Striving for unity within the body of Christ, despite differing preferences in relationship approaches, is crucial. Pridefully looking down on others for making different choices is counterproductive to fostering unity within the body of Christ.

Should we actively seek a spouse or wait for God's provision? Finding a balance between these approaches is key. Frantically searching for a partner solely through our efforts isn't the way, nor should we passively wait for someone to miraculously appear at our doorstep, ready to exchange vows. In Isaac's case, his parents took action to find him a wife, sending a servant to seek a suitable match (Genesis 24). Prayer accompanied this search, and the Lord answered, leading to Isaac and Rebekah's marriage. For Christians seeking a spouse, beginning with prayer, and aligning with God's will is crucial. Delighting in the Lord means finding pleasure in knowing Him and trusting His guidance, allowing His desires to shape our own. Acknowledging God's sovereignty in this process means submitting to His best for us.

Understanding biblical qualities of a godly partner is essential before actively seeking someone. Falling for someone who lacks spiritual compatibility invites heartache. Once aware of these qualities, actively pursuing a spouse while trusting God's timing is vital. Praying for guidance ensures God's leading to the right person. Trusting and waiting on the Lord are important aspects (Proverbs 3:5). Regarding 1 Corinthians 7:27, the context involves a time of persecution where Paul suggests remaining unmarried due to the challenges faced by married couples. However, seeking a spouse isn't inherently wrong, as Paul clarifies in the same passage. God may call some to a life without marriage, as emphasised in 1 Corinthians 7. Accepting this calling aligns with God's specific plan for individuals.

Dear reader,

If you are dating or considering to please consider getting my book: **Before You Say I Do: 21 Consideration to Ponder Before Constructing a Marriage** on Amazon.

THE SACRED UNION:
Exploring the Essence of Marriage

"Marriage is not just a legal contract; it's a sacred covenant, a lifelong commitment to love, honour, and cherish one another, for better or for worse, until death do us part."- Nicholas Robertson

In Genesis 2, God notices that Adam should not live alone, leading to the creation of a woman, establishing the first marriage. This passage sets the blueprint for all future unions: a man and a woman becoming one flesh in a lifelong partnership (Genesis 2:24). The Bible defines marriage as between a man and a woman. God's design intends for a family unit to form from the union of a man and a woman in a committed relationship leading to procreation.

Another principle from Genesis 2 is the lifelong commitment of marriage. The unity between Adam and Eve, forming one flesh, emphasises the permanence of marriage. Their union has no provision for separation, reflecting God's intent for marriage to last a lifetime.

Monogamy is also a key aspect. The scriptural language for "man" and "wife" signifies singular commitment. Though some in Scripture had multiple spouses, God's original plan reflects a union between one man and one woman. Despite cultural shifts redefining marriage, the Bible remains steadfast in its definition: the lifelong union between one man and one woman. However, the Bible doesn't explicitly outline when God considers a couple married, leading to differing viewpoints.

Some argue that legal recognition constitutes marriage, citing biblical calls to obey government laws. However, this view may clash with certain government requirements or lack thereof.

Others see a formal ceremony as God's recognition of marriage. Instances like Jesus attending weddings indicate the acceptability of ceremonies, but they might not be necessary for God's acknowledgment.

A third viewpoint suggests sexual intercourse as the moment of marriage. Yet, this view doesn't align with biblical distinctions between wives and concubines, and it conflicts with the immorality of premarital sex emphasised in Scripture. The story of Isaac and Rebekah doesn't support the idea of mere sexual intercourse constituting marriage. Their union followed a formal process with cultural traditions and

God's confirmation. Considering these perspectives, it's essential for couples to seek reasonable legal recognition, follow cultural practices, and fulfil the physical aspect of union through sexual intimacy.

Dear reader,
If you are dating or married considering to please consider getting our books: **Before You Say I Do: 21 Considerations to Ponder Before Constructing a Marriage** and **After You Say I Do: 21 Consideration for Constructing a Thriving Marriage** on Amazon.

THE DECEPTIVE SNARE:
Understanding the Nature of Pride

"Pride is not just a character flaw; it's a barrier to growth, a stumbling block to humility, and a hindrance to genuine relationships."- Nicholas Robertson

Pride, an intrinsic human trait, bears multifaceted significance across theological, psychological, and philosophical realms. Theologically, pride is defined as an excessive love for one's perceived excellence, identified as a cardinal sin that spawns further transgressions. It stands juxtaposed against the virtue of humility.

In its sinful manifestation, pride propels an individual to overestimate oneself, eclipsing the recognition and appreciation of gifts bestowed by God. The peril of pride lies in its displacement of God from the core of one's spiritual, moral, and temporal existence, positioning the prideful at the epicentre. Should God hold any place in their consciousness, it's solely to inflate one's ego and sense of importance. Pride prompts the individual to sideline God, claiming sole credit for personal accomplishments.

Contrastingly, pride in human psychology encapsulates a sense of satisfaction and self-worth derived from achievements, affiliations, or possessions, fostering confidence and self-respect. However, excessive pride, bordering on vanity or conceit, deviates into an undesirable realm.

Christianity distinguishes between the healthy pride in one's achievements and the sinful pride, also termed "vainglory." The New Testament accentuates glorifying God through good works (Matthew 5:16), while ancient Greek philosophy, as articulated in Plato's "Laws," deems excessive self-love as the root of all offences.

The Bible distinguishes between types of pride: the one detested by God (Proverbs 8:13) and the kind tied to personal accomplishments or admiration for others (Galatians 6:4; 2 Corinthians 7:4). Pride rooted in self-righteousness stands as an impediment to seeking God.

Numerous scriptural instances illustrate the consequences of pride. Proverbs 16:18-19 warns of its harbinger role in destruction and downfall. Lucifer's rebellion against God, driven by pride (Isaiah 14:12-15), epitomises the disastrous outcome of defiance. Pride has historically deterred many from embracing Christ, impeding acknowledgment of personal sin and dependence on divine grace.

Why is pride so egregious? It's an appropriation of God's glory for oneself, failing to acknowledge His role in all accomplishments. Acknowledging God's sovereign role is pivotal, for without His enablement and sustenance, human achievements would remain unattainable. Overcoming pride requires recognition of its addictive and destructive nature. Admitting its presence and confessing it as sin precede the Holy Spirit's corrective work. However, pride's deceit can falsely convince one of humility attained. Scripture offers vivid illustrations of pride's downfall, notably in Nebuchadnezzar's narrative (Daniel 4:30). The king's boastful self-praise incurred divine judgment, leading to a humiliating ordeal. Eventually, humbled, and repentant, he extolled God's sovereignty. To combat pride, one must grasp the vast contrast between human limitations and God's infinite magnitude. Understanding grace, acknowledging God's authorship of all blessings, and praising Him serve as potent tools in humbling oneself. Pride's perilous allure tempts even the most righteous. Its remedy lies in genuine, fervent longing for humility. Awareness of pride's perils and an appreciation for the blessings of humility drive individuals to pursue its attainment.

THE FIERY EMOTION:
Understanding the Nature of Anger

"Anger is not just a fleeting emotion; it's a powerful force that can consume, control, and ultimately destroy if left unchecked." – Nicholas Robertson

Dealing with anger is a vital skill in life, yet reports from Christian counsellors indicate that handling anger remains a challenge for several people seeking counsel. This potent emotion has the capacity to disrupt communication, fracture relationships, and erode both joy and well-being. Unfortunately, many individuals tend to rationalise their anger instead of taking ownership of it. Anger, to varying extents, is a struggle for everyone. Thankfully, God's Word provides principles for handling anger in a manner aligned with godliness and for overcoming sinful anger.

It's crucial to understand that not all anger is sinful. The Bible acknowledges a form of anger known as "righteous indignation," a passion against injustice. God Himself displays anger (Psalm 7:11; Mark 3:5), and it's permissible for believers to experience anger (Ephesians 4:26). In the New Testament, two Greek words denote anger: one signifies "passion" or "energy," while the other denotes being "agitated" or "boiling." Biblically, anger is considered as God-given energy intended to aid in problem-solving. Instances of righteous anger in the Bible include David's reaction to hearing about an injustice (2 Samuel 12) and Jesus' anger over the desecration of worship in Jerusalem's temple (John 2:13-18). Notably, neither instance involved self-defence but rather the defence of others or principles.

Acknowledging that anger over personal injustices is also appropriate is crucial. Anger, in such cases, acts as a warning, indicating violations of boundaries. Even though God cares for each individual, there are times when standing up for oneself becomes necessary, especially for those who have faced abuse or violence. Victims often don't experience immediate anger during trauma; however, as they process through it, anger may emerge. To attain true healing and forgiveness, acknowledging and accepting the injustice is often essential, even if it necessitates experiencing anger. The journey towards acceptance, and even forgiveness, is lengthy but vital for genuine restoration.

However, anger turns sinful when fuelled by pride (James 1:20), distorts God's intentions (1 Corinthians 10:31), or festers without resolution (Ephesians 4:26-27). When anger is aimed at the wrongdoer instead of the problem, when destructive words are unleashed, or when anger spirals out of control, it veers into sinfulness. Refusal to relent, harbouring grudges, or internalising anger leads to emotional distress and often exacerbates unrelated issues. Handling anger biblically involves acknowledging and confessing sinful anger to God and those affected by it (Proverbs 28:13; 1 John 1:9), without making excuses or shifting blame.

Furthermore, understanding God's sovereignty over trials and people who have wronged us aids in dealing with anger. Reflecting on the truth of God's faithfulness and His ability to redeem adverse situations changes our reactions to those who hurt us. Making room for God's justice, rather than retaliating, and responding with love instead of resentment aid in transforming anger into grace-filled actions.

Communication is vital in handling anger biblically. Ephesians 4:15, 25-32 outlines principles: honesty, timeliness, addressing problems, not attacking individuals, and deliberate action instead of impulsive reactions. At times, setting stricter boundaries becomes necessary. Discernment allows us to safeguard ourselves, recognising when certain relationships may not be safe despite our forgiveness.

Finally, addressing our part in the problem and seeking to make changes on our side is imperative. Overcoming a temper is a gradual process, achievable through prayer, scriptural study, and reliance on the Holy Spirit. Although deeply ingrained, with practice, ungodly anger can be replaced by a godly response, glorifying God in our reactions.

Dear reader,

Managing anger is a crucial aspect of emotional maturity and relational health. While anger itself is a natural human emotion, allowing it to control us can lead to harmful consequences. Effective anger management involves acknowledging and understanding the triggers that provoke our anger, whether they be external circumstances or internal frustrations. It requires developing healthy coping mechanisms and communication skills to express our feelings constructively and assertively. This may involve taking a step back to calm down before responding, practicing empathy and understanding towards others, and seeking resolution through peaceful means. Additionally, cultivating self-awareness and practicing forgiveness can help alleviate the underlying resentment and bitterness that fuel anger. Ultimately, managing anger requires a deliberate commitment to self-control, humility, and compassion, enabling us to navigate conflicts and challenges with grace and wisdom.

THE DIGNITY OF LABOUR:
Exploring the Role of Work for Christians

"Work is not just a means to an end; it's a calling, a way to glorify God, serve others, and fulfil our purpose in the world."- Nicholas Robertson

The scriptures in Colossians and Ephesians deliver a resounding message: a call for wholehearted dedication and fervour in work, not merely for earthly masters but as service rendered to the Lord. This constitutes the essence of the Christian work ethic – an earnest obligation to invest our utmost efforts, rooted in gratitude towards the divine gifts bestowed upon us.

From the onset of creation, God wove work into the fabric of existence. Genesis underscores this truth: mankind was initially tasked to cultivate and tend the Garden of Eden, portraying work as an inherent part of God's design. However, after humanity's fall, work metamorphosed into toil, though it remained integral to the 'very good' creation. Throughout the Old Testament, God imparted specific guidelines for work and provision, emphasising the importance of leaving a remnant during harvest for the needy. This divine command underscores the significance of work, not merely providing for the destitute but dignifying them with the opportunity to labour and earn for themselves. Work, therefore, engenders purpose, productivity, and dignity.

The wisdom of Proverbs and Ecclesiastes echoes the importance of diligent labour. These scriptures extol the virtue of hard work, issuing warnings against slothfulness and idle talk. Ecclesiastes elucidates the philosophy of unflinching commitment in every endeavour.

The New Testament further illuminates the Christian approach to work, advocating that refusal to work ought to lead to deprivation. The teachings of Paul accentuate the value of industriousness, exemplifying diligence, and conscientiousness. Paul's example resonates through his tireless efforts to ensure self-sufficiency while ministering.
For Christians, work isn't merely a task but an integral facet of life, to be approached as a divine gift. Working earnestly, untainted by grievances, is akin to rendering service to the benevolent Lord, fostering an opportunity to display faithfulness and diligence, thereby serving as a testament to others.

However, the Bible does not endorse an unhealthy obsession with work. The scriptures caution against the pursuit of worldly wealth to the detriment of spiritual growth, reminding believers that glorifying God remains the primary goal. Moreover, work should not endanger health or jeopardise familial bonds. God, above all, values a relationship with His children more than their work. God's wisdom permeates the concept of rest, manifested in the Sabbath. The omnipotent Creator's example of rest on the seventh day emphasises the importance of intervals of repose. While the specific Sabbath laws may not apply to believers today, the principle of rest remains pertinent – a divine gift for humanity's well-being. Hence, while Christians are enjoined to uphold an unwavering work ethic, they are also encouraged to embrace moments of rest as a divine endowment. This balanced approach towards work and rest honours God, ensuring that work is performed dutifully without overshadowing the need for reprieve and communion with God.

Dear reader,

The dignity of work is a fundamental principle that upholds the inherent value and worth of every individual's labour and contribution to society recognising that work is not merely a means of earning a living but also a source of personal fulfilment, dignity, and purpose. Work purposefully!

RESPONSIBLE GUARDIANSHIP:
Understanding the Concept of Stewardship

"Stewardship is not just about managing resources; it's about recognising that everything we have belongs to God and using it wisely for His purposes."- Nicholas Robertson

Understanding what the Bible teaches about stewardship begins at the very genesis: "In the beginning God created the heavens and the earth" (Genesis 1:1). This declaration underscores God's absolute ownership over everything. Neglecting this foundational truth is like misaligning the top button of a shirt—it disrupts the entire alignment. The doctrine of stewardship lacks relevance and coherence without acknowledging God as the Creator and ultimate owner. Embracing this truth is pivotal in grasping the essence of stewardship.

Stewardship, as per the Bible, defines the relationship between humanity and God, portraying God as the owner and humans as managers. God appoints us as co-workers, entrusting us with the administration of all aspects of life. The apostle Paul articulates this concept, stating, "For we are

God's fellow workers; you are God's field, God's building" (1 Corinthians 3:9). Understanding this foundational premise allows us to value not only our possessions but, more significantly, human life itself. Stewardship defines our divine purpose, a partnership with God in His eternal redemptive mission (Matthew 28:19-20). It's not about God taking from us but rather bestowing His abundant gifts upon His people.

In the New Testament, two Greek words encapsulate the essence of our English term "stewardship." The first, "epitropos," refers to "manager, foreman, or steward." It was also used in terms of "governor or procurator" and occasionally as "guardian" in Galatians 4:1-2. The second term, "oikonomos," similarly signifies "steward, manager, or administrator" and appears more frequently. It pertains mainly to household management or administration of affairs. In Paul's writings, "oikonomos" carries profound significance, illustrating his responsibility to preach the gospel as a divine trust (1 Corinthians 9:17). He views his calling as the administration of God's grace, revealing the divine mystery in Christ (Ephesians 3:2). Paul envisions God as the master of a vast household, skilfully managing it through him as an obedient servant of Jesus Christ. Paul emphasises that the stewardship we are entrusted with upon being called into Christ's body doesn't rely on our own strength or abilities. The power, inspiration, and growth in managing our lives must stem from God through the Holy Spirit within us; otherwise, our efforts are in vain, merely human endeavours. Thus, our strength to please God originates solely from Christ: "I can do all things through Christ who strengthens me" (Philippians 4:13 NJKV). Paul acknowledges, "But by the grace of God I am what I am, and His grace to me was not without effect. No, I worked harder than all of them—yet not I, but the grace of God that was with me" (1 Corinthians 15:10). Stewardship extends beyond managing finances or paying tithes. It encompasses managing time, possessions, environment, health, and more. It's the obedient expression of one's belief in God's sovereignty, inspiring followers of Christ to act. Paul's stewardship, for instance, involved proclaiming the entrusted gospel truth.

At its core, stewardship signifies practical obedience in managing everything under our control, acknowledging that we and all we possess belong to God. It's the consecration of self and possessions in service to God. Stewardship signifies that we are managers of what belongs to God, under His constant authority. Being faithful stewards means acknowledging that we belong to Christ, who sacrificed Himself for us.

Ultimately, stewardship prompts this crucial question: Who is the Lord of my life—myself or Christ? In essence, it reflects our complete obedience to God and Jesus Christ, our Lord and Saviour.

Dear reader,
Stewardship is the responsible and ethical management or care of resources whether they are natural, financial, or organisational. It involves the careful and sustainable use of resources, with the understanding that they are entrusted to us and that we have a duty to preserve and enhance them for present and future generations. Additionally, it encompasses the idea that everything we have, including our time, talents, possessions, and the Earth itself, is a gift from God, and we are called to use these resources wisely and in accordance with God's will. Be a good steward of the gifts you possess.

THE JOY OF GENEROSITY:
Exploring the Meaning of Giving

"True giving is not measured by the amount given, but by the heart behind the gift—a heart that overflows with love, compassion, and a desire to bless others."- Nicholas Robertson

The act of giving, as outlined in the Bible, holds significant importance within Christian teachings. Jesus emphasised the correlation between one's heart and their approach to finances, underscoring that where our treasure lies, our heart follows suit (Matthew 6:21). This principle urges introspection into our spending patterns and how our financial resources reflect our devotion to God's work through giving.

The Bible provides foundational principles guiding our understanding and practice of giving:

- **Divine Ownership:** Scriptures affirm that everything, including money, belongs to God. Psalm 24:1 asserts this truth, while Proverbs 22:2 stresses that the Lord is the creator of all. Acknowledging this, shapes our perspective on finances and prompts us to use God's resources according to His intentions.

- **Giving as Worship:** Colossians 3:17 extends the call to honour God in all our actions to our financial decisions. This includes ensuring that our spending aligns with glorifying and honouring God, involving contributions to church ministries and acts of charity.

- **Biblical Command:** The Bible directs believers to give to support God's work. 1 Corinthians 16:1–2 specifically addresses this, encouraging consistent contributions to ministry as a Christian duty.

- **Attitude in Giving:** Giving should reflect thoughtfulness, sacrificial generosity, and joy. 1 Corinthians 16:2 encourages thoughtful giving based on personal discernment rather than reluctance or obligation. The Scriptures highlight the joy of giving and the blessings it brings, as seen in 2 Corinthians 9:6–7 and the sacrificial example of the Macedonians (2 Corinthians 8:1–9).In the Old Testament, the Israelites were commanded to allocate a portion of their income, including tithes (10 percent) and additional offerings, to support the Levites, fund religious celebrations, and assist the poor. However, the New Testament aligns more with freewill offerings, reflecting heartfelt gratitude to God.

- **Quiet Generosity:** Jesus cautioned against showy giving and stressed the value of discreet, unobtrusive generosity. The Scriptures emphasise giving in secret, without seeking recognition, assuring a reward from God instead of human applause (Matthew 6:3–4).

- **Divine Promises:** Sacrificial and generous giving leads to blessings. Scriptures affirm that generosity invites divine blessings and rewards, both in this life and the next (2 Corinthians 9:6, Proverbs 22:9, Luke 6:38). While earthly prosperity isn't the focus, believers trust in God's promise to bless their sacrificial giving.

Dear reader,

Paul, in Philippians 4:18, commended the Philippians for their generous financial support, describing it as an offering pleasing to God. Likewise, believers today honour God through faithful stewardship and generous giving.

HONOURING GOD WITH OUR FINANCES:
Exploring Biblical Principles of Tithing

"Tithing is not just about giving a portion of our income; it's about acknowledging God's ownership of all we have and expressing our gratitude and trust in Him through faithful stewardship." – Nicholas Robertson

Tithe denotes giving ten percent. In the Old Testament, the Israelites were instructed to tithe, as laid out in various passages (Leviticus 27:30-32; Numbers 18:21-28; Deuteronomy 12:6-17; 14:22-28; 26:12-14). But the real query behind "What does the Bible say about tithing?" often revolves around whether God mandates Christians to give 10% of their income to the church. The Bible, across both Old and New Testaments, extensively covers the concept of giving. Therefore, pastors shouldn't shy away from discussing giving or tithing. However, the pressure on pastors to drive giving has led to numerous misapplications and misinterpretations of biblical tithing. Some churches display annual lists of top givers, while others scrutinise members' tax returns to confirm a 10% tithe. There are instances where tithing becomes a legalistic requirement for salvation, or financial difficulties are linked directly to a lack of tithing. Even though pastors should maintain sound biblical interpretations irrespective of financial pressures, sometimes these pressures can influence interpretations. The temptation to encourage more generous giving can be substantial when a pastor's capacity to support their family hinges on garnering contributions. Sadly, some pastors, aware that the New Testament doesn't advocate tithing and that Jesus fulfilled the Law, still preach tithing as a Christian obligation. This should not be the case; accurate teaching based on the Word is imperative (2 Timothy 2:15; 4:2), allowing the Holy Spirit to convict.

While most churches or denominations endorse tithing to some extent, the standard of ten percent predominantly stems from the Old Testament Law. However, biblically, this doesn't align with true tithing as the Old Testament prescribed multiple tithes, almost totalling 25% of income for the Israelites. Crucially, the Old Testament Law isn't applicable to Christian tithing. Jesus fulfilled the Law, including its tithing laws (Romans 10:4; Galatians 3:23-25; Ephesians 2:15). The New Testament emphasises giving (1 Corinthians 16:2; 2 Corinthians 9:7), but apart from a mention in relation to the Old Testament Law in Matthew 23:23, it doesn't explicitly discuss tithing. There's no fixed amount recommended or required for giving in the New Testament. Christians are urged to give generously, sacrificially, and joyfully, embracing the liberty in Christ without any mandated tithing obligation.

What is the biblical stance on tithing for Christians?
If led by God to tithe, then do so. However, tithing shouldn't be seen as a legalistic demand. Giving is integral to Christian life, but there's no prescribed amount. It's challenging, but faith entails sacrificial giving rather than adhering to a checklist of obligations.

Dear reader,
Faith calls us to a life beyond legalism, embracing a spirit of sacrificial generosity.

UNMASKING THE ENEMY:
Exploring the Identity of Satan

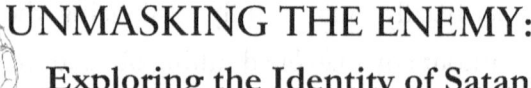

"Satan is not just a fictional character or a symbol of evil; he is a real and formidable adversary, seeking to deceive, destroy, and derail God's plans for humanity." – Nicholas Robertson

Various beliefs about Satan range from the comical to the conceptual—from a little horned figure coaxing people into sin to representing the embodiment of evil. Yet, the Bible offers a defined understanding of Satan and his impact on our lives. The Bible characterises Satan as an angelic being who, due to sin, fell from his heavenly position and is now in complete opposition to God, striving to obstruct His plans. Originally created as a holy angel, Satan is possibly referred to as Lucifer in Isaiah 14:12. Described in Ezekiel 28:12-14 as a cherub, seemingly the highest among created angels, he grew proud in his beauty and status, aspiring to a throne higher than God's (Isaiah 14:13-14; Ezekiel 28:15; 1 Timothy 3:6), leading to his downfall.

Satan became the ruler of this world and the prince of the power of the air (John 12:31; 2 Corinthians 4:4; Ephesians 2:2). He embodies accusation (Revelation 12:10), temptation (Matthew 4:3; 1 Thessalonians 3:5), and deception (Genesis

3; 2 Corinthians 4:4; Revelation 20:3). His name signifies "adversary" or "one who opposes," while his title, the devil, means "slanderer." Although banished from heaven, he persists in seeking to exalt himself above God. He counterfeits God's actions, aiming to gain worship and incite opposition to God's kingdom. Satan stands as the root behind every false cult and worldly religion. He will go to any length to oppose God and His followers. Yet, Satan's fate is determined—an eternity in the lake of fire (Revelation 20:10).

Satan, depicted in the Bible as an angelic adversary of God and consequently an enemy of God's followers, chose rebellion against the Lord, leading numerous other angels in this defiance (Ezekiel 28:15; Isaiah 14:12–17). In the Garden of Eden, he tempted Eve, inducing Adam to join her in sin, plunging humanity into a curse (Genesis 3:16–19; Romans 5:12). Identified as both a serpent and dragon in Scripture (Genesis 3:1; Revelation 12:9), Satan is characterised as a murderer and the father of lies. He advocates false doctrines and craftily holds unbelievers in spiritual bondage (John 8:44; 2 Corinthians 4:4; 11:14; 1 Timothy 4:1). Although the Bible presents various details about Satan, it's equally crucial to establish what it doesn't mention about him. Numerous misconceptions surround the devil, including these:

- Satan is not a personal entity but merely represents a force of evil.

- He stands equal to God, creating a form of dualism.
- He presides over and governs hell.
- He possesses unrestricted power to do as he pleases.
- He is omnipresent.
- He received a ransom from Jesus when Christ died on the cross.

All these views are inaccurate and lack biblical support. False notions about Satan arise from various sources. For instance, the belief that Satan equals God's opposite emerged from Zoroastrianism's dualism. The idea that Jesus died to pay a ransom to Satan was theorised by Origen. John Milton's Paradise Lost, not the Bible, portrays Satan as the ruler of hell (I:261–263). The Bible furnishes the following insights about Satan:

- Satan is a personal entity, possessing intellect, emotions, and a will (Job 1; Matthew 4:1–12).
- He is a created being and is not on par with God (Ezekiel 28:15).
- Satan does not reign over hell; hell was fashioned as punishment for Satan and his demons (Matthew 25:41).
- Satan does not reside in hell; instead, the Bible depicts him entering heaven and traversing the earth (Job 1:6–7).
- The devil can only act within God's allowance (Job 1:12).
- Satan is not omnipresent. However, he oversees a legion of demons referred to as "the powers of this dark world and . . . the spiritual forces of evil in the heavenly realms"

(Ephesians 6:12), utilising this network to tempt and deceive people.
- He actively endeavours to nullify the impact of God's Word in people's hearts (Matthew 13:3–4, 19) and blinds the understanding of nonbelievers, preventing them from grasping the gospel (2 Corinthians 4:4).

The Bible advises Christians to be vigilant of Satan's schemes: "Be alert and of sober mind. Your enemy the devil prowls around like a roaring lion looking for someone to devour" (1 Peter 5:8). Believers must resist him with sobriety, vigilance, and unwavering faith, recognising his intentions to tempt and render them unproductive for the Lord (2 Corinthians 2:11). When confronted with temptation, believers are encouraged to yield to the Lord, resist Satan, and he will flee (James 4:7).

Besides tempting, Satan is also "the accuser of our brothers" (Revelation 12:10, ESV). He takes pleasure in listing believers' sins, but our Advocate, Jesus Christ, nullifies these accusations by paying the price for our sins (1 John 2:1–2). Christians can trust their salvation because Jesus accomplished this through His death and resurrection (Ephesians 2:8–9).

Satan is designated as the "god of this age" (2 Corinthians 4:4) and possesses dominion over the world and its systems (John

12:31; 1 John 5:19). However, his authority will not last indefinitely. During the tribulation, Satan will deceive the masses and raise the Antichrist, who will reign for seven years (Revelation 13:5–8). As Satan has always craved worship, this will be part of his deceit, as many will worship him during that period (Revelation 13:4). He will also attempt to annihilate the remnant of Israel but will not succeed (Revelation 12:13–16). Ultimately, at the tribulation's conclusion, Jesus will return, the Antichrist and false prophet will be cast into the lake of fire, and Satan will be incarcerated for 1,000 years (Revelation 19:19–20; 20:1–3). Following his release, Satan will incite a final rebellion (Revelation 20:7–9). Finally, he will be cast into the lake of fire, eternally tormented for his rebellion and malevolent acts (Revelation 20:10).

Dear reader,

While Satan's dominion over the world might seem impregnable, he cannot withstand the power of our Saviour and Lord, Jesus Christ.

CULTIVATING EXCELLENCE:
Nurturing Strong Work Ethic

"Excellence in work is not just about achieving perfection; it's about consistently giving our best, embracing challenges, and continually striving for improvement."- Nicholas Robertson

In everything set them an example by doing what is good. In your teaching show integrity, seriousness and soundness of speech that cannot be condemned, so that those who oppose you may be ashamed because they have nothing bad to say about us (Titus 2:7-8)

This speaks to character: Character is defined as the strength of the moral fibre. A.W. Tozer described the character as "the excellence of moral beings." As the excellence of gold is its purity and the excellence of art is its beauty, so the excellence of man is his character. Persons of character are noted for their honesty, ethics, and charity. Descriptions such as "man of principle" and "woman of integrity" are assertions of character. A lack of character is a moral deficiency, and persons lacking character tend to behave dishonestly, unethically, and uncharitably.

Titus had to be more than a teacher; he also had to be an example. His guidance to others could not be taken seriously if he himself was not walking after the Lord. Titus had to be an example in doctrinal stability and integrity. If he wasn't comfortably settled in his understanding of the Scriptures, he wasn't ready to lead. that one who is an opponent may be ashamed: So that your accusers will be embarrassed, having nothing to hold against you. Jesus could say to an angry mob, "Which of you convicts Me of sin?" (John 8:46)

"The clause **having nothing to say** means having nothing evil to report concerning us: not, as purported by the English versions, having no evil thing to say."

Remember, excellence is not on break. In a world filled with challenges, uncertainties, and moments of respite, it's easy to feel tempted to lower our standards to take a break from our pursuit of excellence. However, true excellence is not a part-time endeavour; it is a commitment that transcends circumstances.

As we navigate the intricacies of our lives, both personally and professionally, let us remember that excellence is a constant companion, urging us to rise above mediocrity. It beckons us to embrace a mindset that seeks the best in every situation and to put forth our best effort regardless of the challenges that may come our way.

Excellence is not a destination; it is a continuous journey. It's the unwavering dedication to continuous improvement, the refusal to settle for anything less than our very best. When faced with adversity, let us not retreat into complacency but rather use those moments to sharpen our skills, refine our character, and emerge stronger than before. In our relationships, let excellence guide our actions. Let us be known for the kindness we show, the empathy we extend, and the integrity we uphold. In our work, let excellence be the hallmark of our efforts, a testimony to our commitment to craftsmanship and diligence. The pursuit of excellence is not without its challenges, but it is in overcoming these challenges that we truly shine. It is in those moments when we choose to persevere, to push through difficulties, that we demonstrate the resilience and strength that excellence demands.

So, my dear friends, let us embrace the truth that excellence is not on break. It is a constant, a guiding light that illuminates our path even in the darkest of times. As we journey forward, may we carry with us the unwavering commitment to excellence in all that we do, knowing that it is through this pursuit that we leave a lasting impact on the world around us. May the spirit of excellence guide our thoughts, actions, and aspirations today and always.

Dear reader,

For more information on cultivating an excellent attitude, consider getting my book: Positive Vibration: **Navigating Through Difficult Times**

THE SACRED FEAST:
Exploring the Meaning of Holy Communion

"Holy Communion is not just a religious ritual; it's a sacred encounter, a tangible reminder of Christ's sacrifice, and a profound expression of our unity as believers."- Nicholas Robertson

The Christian practice often referred to as "communion" finds its origin in Jesus' establishment of an ordinance during the Last Supper with His disciples. It serves as an outward expression of believers' affection for and fellowship with Christ, a remembrance of Jesus' sacrificial atonement, and an anticipation of sharing in His kingdom. Also known as the Lord's supper or table, communion holds significant importance among Christians.

The Last Supper took place just before Judas Iscariot's betrayal of Jesus in the Garden of Gethsemane. Jesus gathered His disciples in an upper room to commemorate the Passover. However, the occasion unveiled another purpose. During the meal, Jesus took bread, gave thanks, broke it, and told His disciples, "Take and eat; this is my body." He then offered them a cup, giving thanks again, and said, "Drink from it, all of you. This is my blood of the covenant, poured out for many for the forgiveness of sins. I will not drink from this fruit of the vine until I drink it new with you in my Father's kingdom" (Matthew 26:26–29).

These words held familiarity for the disciples who should have recalled Jesus' earlier teachings. He had previously spoken to a crowd about eating His flesh and drinking His blood as symbols of eternal life, a notion that proved challenging for many to accept (John 6:53–66).

Following Jesus' death, resurrection, and ascension, the early church adhered to His commandment, practicing communion as Jesus had instructed. The Apostle Paul emphasised fellowship during communion, highlighting its unifying effect among believers. He also cautioned against approaching communion with flippancy or dishonour, stressing the need for self-examination before partaking (1 Corinthians 10:16–17, 11:26–29).

Communion stands as one of two ordinances in the church, its frequency not explicitly specified in the Bible. It serves as a time for reflection on individual sinfulness, the necessity for forgiveness, and Christ's grace displayed on the cross (John 3:16). By partaking together, Christians symbolise their unity with each other and with Christ, recollecting His sacrifice and anticipating His return. Communion embodies a shared spiritual connection and echoes Jesus' desire for unity among believers (Philippians 2:1; John 17:22–23).

Dear reader,
Holy Communion serves as a tangible expression of believers' faith, unity, and fellowship with Christ and with one another, as well as a means of receiving spiritual nourishment, grace, and empowerment for Christian living.

THE STRENGTH OF MEEKNESS:
Understanding the Virtue of Humility

"Meekness is not weakness; it's the quiet strength of a surrendered soul, grounded in humility and empowered by grace."- Nicholas Robertson

Meekness encapsulates an attitude or characteristic of the heart where one willingly accepts and submits, without resistance, to the desires and will of another. It's an active and intentional embrace of unfavourable circumstances, understood as part of a broader panorama. Meekness isn't about resigning to destiny or passively succumbing to events—such a response holds little virtue. Nonetheless, the similarity in outward appearance between resignation and meekness has led to the misconception that what was once seen as a virtue is now perceived as a flaw in modern society.

The patient endurance and hopeful outlook amidst adverse situations distinguish a person practicing meekness. Externally, they may seem vulnerable and feeble, yet internally, they exhibit resilience and strength. Meekness doesn't denote weakness but rather defines the strength of individuals positioned in a state of vulnerability, persevering without giving in. The use of the Greek term, particularly in reference to animals, clarifies this notion. When applied to wild animals, it implies "tame." This doesn't suggest a loss of strength but rather an acquired ability to control destructive instincts, enabling them to coexist harmoniously with others.

The Beatitudes in the Sermon on the Mount, among which the third declares, "Blessed are the meek, for they will inherit the earth" (Matthew 5:5), resonate with Psalm 37:11, affirming, "The meek will inherit the land and enjoy peace and prosperity." But what does it truly mean to be "blessed" as the meek? To understand this, we must grasp the essence of "blessed." The Greek term translated as "blessed" can also denote "happy." The notion conveyed is that one finds joy in meekness. This blessedness isn't merely earthly happiness but rather spiritual fulfilment from God's perspective.

Additionally, comprehending "meekness" is crucial. The Greek term "praeis" denotes mildness, a gentle spirit, or humility. This same root appears in other New Testament passages like James 1:21 and James 3:13. Meekness embodies humility towards God and others—it's possessing the right or power to act but choosing restraint for another's benefit. Paul advocates for meekness, urging believers to lead lives that reflect their divine calling, marked by complete humility, gentleness, and patience towards each other (Ephesians 4:1–2).

Meekness mirrors the humility exemplified by Jesus Christ. Philippians 2:6–8 illustrates this: "[Jesus], though being in very nature God, did not consider equality with God something to be used to His own advantage; rather, He made Himself nothing by taking the very nature of a servant, being made in human likeness. And being found in appearance as a man, He humbled Himself by becoming obedient to death—even death on a cross!" Though possessing divine prerogatives, Jesus submitted Himself to "death on a cross" for our sake—a supreme demonstration of meekness. Notably, meekness characterised revered leaders in the Old Testament. Numbers 12:3 notes that Moses "was very meek, more than all people who were on the face of the earth" (ESV). Believers are called to convey the gospel message with gentleness and meekness. First Peter 3:15 counsels, "Always be prepared to give an answer to everyone who asks you to give the reason for the hope that you have. But do this with gentleness and respect." The King James Version translates "gentleness" here as "meekness."

A person acquainted with Christ as their personal Saviour will inevitably grow in meekness. It may seem paradoxical, but Jesus' pledge holds true meekness brings happiness or blessedness. Living humbly and relinquishing rights for others' benefit mirrors the attitude of Jesus Christ. Meekness also enhances our effectiveness in sharing the gospel.

Dear reader,
Pursuing power and prestige isn't the route to blessedness; rather, it's the path of meekness.

BALANCE AND MODERATION:
Exploring the Concept of Temperance

"Temperance is the mastery of self, the disciplined restraint that allows us to navigate life's challenges with grace and wisdom."- Nicholas Robertson

Temperance, the art of moderation in thought, word, and deed, reflects an individual's ability to exercise self-control and restraint in his/her passions and actions. Frequently associated with curtailing alcohol consumption, the concept gained prominence during the late 19th and early 20th centuries as part of the "temperance movement," aimed at restricting or eradicating the sale and use of alcohol. In the New Testament, temperance emerges as a recurring theme, particularly concerning character development.

Ephesians 5:18 subtly alludes to temperance regarding alcohol, urging against inebriation, advocating instead for being filled with the Holy Spirit. The absence of moderation in alcohol consumption hinders the Spirit's influence over one's decisions, allowing alcohol to take control. This principle extends beyond alcohol to encompass any aspect lacking temperance. For Christians, the standard is clear: only the Holy Spirit should govern our lives (Galatians 5:25). Unchecked desires, whether for alcohol, food, lust, or greed, become the functional idols guiding our actions.

Temperance, or self-control, stands as one of the fruits of the Spirit within believers (Galatians 5:22). Without self-control, living in a godly manner and pleasing the Lord becomes unattainable, as our flesh incessantly craves self-gratification (Romans 7:21–25). Romans 13:14 urges believers not to make allowances for fleshly desires and their accompanying lusts. However, misconceptions often arise, assuming that temperance permits dabbling in sin as long as one is not overtaken by it. This misinterpretation negates the essence of the verse, which advocates for cautiousness and wisdom. A desire to please the Lord necessitates a deliberate avoidance of anything hinting at evil. Leading a temperate life doesn't provide a license for minor transgressions; it demands abstaining from sin altogether.

Paul delineates biblical temperance in 1 Corinthians 9:27, stressing discipline over his body to prevent disqualification despite preaching to others. Recognising the potential of the flesh to undermine his ministry, Paul denied his flesh its cravings to cultivate a robust character. Present-day headlines often serve as cautionary reminders, illustrating the repercussions of engaging in Christian ministry without exercising temperance. When Christian leaders falter, it frequently traces back to a lack of self-control and personal discipline.

Dear reader,

Temperance's antithesis lies in self-indulgence. The development of lazy attitudes in one sphere often proliferates into other areas. In contrast, maintaining physical, mental, and spiritual self-control equips individuals for greater efficacy in representing Christ (Matthew 28:19–20; 1 Corinthians 10:31).

ENDURANCE IN ADVERSITY:
Understanding the Notion of Longsuffering

"Longsuffering is not just enduring trials; it's persevering with patience and grace, trusting in God's timing and purpose even in the midst of adversity."- Nicholas Robertson

Longsuffering is simply the art of patience. Longsuffering, often misconstrued as simply "suffering long," carries a deeper connotation in the Biblical context. The word "longsuffering" in the Bible originates from two Greek words, meaning "long" and "temper" — essentially signifying "long-tempered." It encapsulates the notion of exercising self-restraint when provoked to anger. A longsuffering individual refrains from immediate retaliation or retribution; they possess a 'long fuse,' displaying patient forbearance. Longsuffering intertwines with mercy (1 Peter 3:20) and hope (1 Thessalonians 1:3), refusing to surrender to circumstances or succumb to trials.

At its core, longsuffering emanates from God Himself, an integral part of His character (Exodus 34:6; Numbers 14:18–20; Psalm 86:15; Romans 2:4; 1 Peter 3:9; 2 Peter 3:15). God's patience extends towards sinners, yet it can reach its limit, demonstrated in events like the destruction of Sodom and Gomorrah (Genesis 18—19) and the exile of Israel (2 Kings 17:1-23; 24:17—25:30).

Upon believing in Jesus Christ, a believer receives the divine life of God, infused with His nature (2 Peter 1:4). This life manifests specific characteristics, or 'fruit,' as the believer yields to the Holy Spirit residing within. Among these godly attributes listed in Galatians 5:22-23 is "longsuffering," termed as "patience" in some translations like the New American Standard Bible. Longsuffering is an expected trait for all believers (Ephesians 4:2; Colossians 1:11; 3:12).

Consider the transformative impact of longsuffering in individual, familial, church, and workplace relationships. The innate human tendency to react swiftly to provocations often results in unkind retorts and unforgiving attitudes. Through obedience to the Holy Spirit, a Christ-believer can reject retaliation and instead display a forgiving and patient disposition. Just as God exercises longsuffering towards us, we are implored to exhibit the same towards others (Ephesians 4:30-32).

Dear reader,

The ultimate illustration of God's longsuffering is His enduring wait for individuals to embrace faith in Jesus Christ. God's desire is for none to perish but for all to repent (2 Peter 3:9). Have you made the decision to believe in the sacrificial death and resurrection of Jesus Christ for forgiveness and eternal life? If not, reflect on Romans 10:9–13.

THE LANGUAGE OF THE HEART:
Examining the Meaning of Love

"Love is not just a feeling; it's a choice, an action, a commitment to cherish, support, and uplift one another through every season of life." – Nicholas Robertson

Defining love proves challenging, embedded in the multifaceted ways individuals experience it. Love encompasses personal affection, sexual attraction, platonic admiration, loyalty, benevolence, and even worshipful adoration. To truly fathom its essence, we must trace its origin. The Bible establishes love as an attribute emanating from God. In the English language, the term "love" involves a spectrum of meanings, incorporating everything from adoration for pancakes to reverence for parents, each with distinct nuances. In contrast, the ancient languages of the Bible, Hebrew, and Greek, employ distinct words to articulate different forms of love. These languages delineate among sexual, brotherly, familial love, and the divine love shared between God and His creation.

The Hebrew word 'yada' and the Greek word 'eros' denote sexual love. In Genesis 38, Judah engages with a woman he assumes to be a prostitute. The original Hebrew term in verse 26, 'yada,' implies "to know" or "to have sexual intercourse with." Conversely, the Greek word 'eros' finds no context in the New Testament.

Another form of love is the affection shared between close friends, devoid of sexual connotations—a love evident in friendships. The Hebrew 'ahabah' represents this type, as seen in the bond between David and Jonathan in 1 Samuel 20:17. In Greek, 'phileo' denotes brotherly affection, referred to in John 15:19, Romans 12:10, and Hebrews 13:1.

Family or tribal love is represented by the Hebrew 'ahabah' signifying deep affection, while the Greek 'storge' mirrors this sentiment. The Hebrew 'ahabah' is widespread in the Old Testament due to its expansive meaning, while the Greek 'storge' appears negatively as 'astorgos,' meaning "without natural love," as noted in 2 Timothy 3:3.

Lastly, the Hebrew 'chesed' and the Greek 'agape' symbolise God's love towards His chosen ones. 'Chesed' signifies "steadfast love" or "lovingkindness," typified in Numbers 14:18. 'Agape' reflects God's goodwill and self-sacrificial commitment, demonstrated through an unwavering, unconditional love, akin to 'chesed.' This form of love is pivotal in fulfilling the greatest commandment (Matthew 22:37) and is to be embraced by Jesus' followers in their service to others (Matthew 22:39; John 13:34).

Dear reader,

At its core, love embodies emotions and actions arising from concern for another's well-being. It comprises affection, compassion, care, and self-sacrifice. Originating in the Triune Godhead's eternal relationship, love constitutes a unique aspect of humanity's identity as image-bearers of God. While a pet owner might cherish her dog, the reciprocation of true love remains absent. Animals lack the capacity for human-like love, a distinction rooted in our creation in God's image. Love finds its epitome in God's demonstration: "This is love: not that we loved God, but that He loved us and sent His Son as an atoning sacrifice for our sins. Dear friends, since God so loved us, we also ought to love one another" (1 John 4:9–11, 19).

JOURNEYING IN TRUST:
Understanding the Meaning of Walking by Faith

"To walk by faith is to step into the unknown with confidence, trusting in God's guidance and provision even when the path ahead seems uncertain."- Nicholas Robertson

Faith, the basis of belief, loyalty, and trust in God, embodies a firm conviction in the absence of tangible proof. When the apostle Paul exhorts the Corinthians to "walk by faith and not by sight" (2 Corinthians 5:7), he beckons them to tread a path guided by their unwavering trust in God's word and promises.

Walking signifies not standing still but continually moving forward, even in uncertainty, where the full trajectory remains concealed. As Martin Luther King Jr. poignantly articulated, "Faith is taking the first step, even when you don't see the staircase." It's an understanding that propels us to keep moving in a direction divinely ordained, guided by the Word of God and the assurance of His promises.

Romans 8:28 assures us that all events ultimately work together for the good of those who love God and are aligned with His purpose.

Matthew 6:23 highlights the necessity of having a clear perspective, for the eyes' clarity reflects the soul's illumination.

2 Peter 3:9 reassures that God is patient, desiring repentance, and salvation for all.

Psalm 84:11 underlines that the Lord is a protector and provider for those who walk in righteousness.

Nevertheless, walking by faith does not promise a journey devoid of challenges. Rather, it necessitates wholeheartedly trusting God to guide us through every obstacle toward a favourable outcome.

This journey doesn't grant us the authority to alter God's plan; instead, it invites us into partnership with Him, aligning ourselves with His divine will. Just as Israel was led through the wilderness instead of a familiar, easier route, faith may steer us along unfamiliar paths.

Faith doesn't always grant our desires or ensure a pleasant journey. Isaac, amidst a severe famine, stood in the promised land, affirming that faith doesn't always bring immediate relief but instead leads us in trust towards God's promises.

Paul, in his dialogue with the Corinthians, propounds the temporary nature of our earthly bodies. He assures us that despite the transient state of our physical existence, we possess a profound, eternal hope of being with God.

Our bodies, likened to tents, are merely temporal dwellings for our spirits. Even if these perish, our eternal hope lies in being eternally united with God.

In refuting the Greek philosophers' belief in bodiless existence, Paul underscores our future transformation. Our perishable bodies will don incorruptibility, exchanging mortality for immortality, as outlined in 1 Corinthians 15:53.

Dear reader,
The present discomforts, when viewed through the lens of faith, appear as momentary afflictions, ushering us toward an eternal glory that outweighs the transient adversities of our earthly existence. So let us traverse this earthly realm, restricted by its limitations, while nurturing a steadfast belief in an extraordinary future—a life without boundaries or constraints. This journey, walked by faith, holds the promise of an eternal existence beyond measure.

THE LANGUAGE OF THE SPIRIT:
Exploring the Gift of Speaking in Tongues

"The gift of speaking in tongues is a divine expression of prayer, worship, and intimacy with God, allowing the Spirit to intercede on our behalf in ways beyond our understanding."

The initial instance of speaking in tongues traces back to the event of Pentecost, vividly detailed in Acts 2:1–4. As the apostles shared the gospel, astonishingly, each listener heard the message in their native language. This miraculous occurrence was a demonstration of the gift of tongues—speaking in languages unknown to the speaker but understood by the audience. This aligns with the literal translation of the Greek term for "tongues," which means "languages."

In the letters to the Corinthians, the apostle Paul delves into the subject of miraculous gifts, particularly highlighting the necessity of interpreting tongues. He stresses the importance of intelligible communication, asserting that speaking in tongues serves its purpose when interpreted for the listeners' understanding (1 Corinthians 14:6).

For the benefit of the congregation, Paul accentuates the significance of interpreting tongues. Those gifted with interpretation could grasp the message conveyed in an unknown language, allowing them to relay it comprehensibly to others. The apostle urges those speaking in tongues to pray for the ability to interpret, affirming the superiority of intelligible communication over incomprehensible utterances (1 Corinthians 14:13, 19).

Regarding the continuity of the gift of tongues, interpretations vary. Some argue that 1 Corinthians 13:8 hints at the cessation of tongues, correlating it with the advent of the "perfect" in 1 Corinthians 13:10. Others connect passages from Isaiah and Joel to suggest that tongues signified God's impending judgment and thus ceased following Israel's rejection of Jesus as Messiah.

Scripture doesn't definitively state the cessation of the gift of tongues. If this gift were active today, it should align with biblical parameters—manifesting in real, coherent languages for the purpose of conveying God's Word across linguistic barriers and practised orderly in the church. The absence of verifiable occurrences of tongues as described in the New

Testament raises questions about its contemporary existence within the church.

Dear reader,

While God can indeed bestow the gift of tongues for cross-lingual communication, the apparent rarity of its occurrence today raises uncertainty. Though it would immensely benefit missions and evangelism, the majority who claim the gift often do not adhere to the biblical guidelines. These considerations lead to the query of whether the gift of tongues has ceased or has become exceedingly rare in God's current design for the church.

HEALING BROKEN BONDS:
Exploring the Meaning of Reconciliation

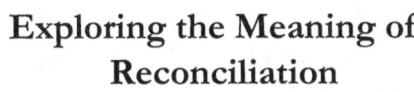

"Reconciliation is not just about restoring relationships; it's about healing wounds, bridging divides, and rebuilding trust, creating a pathway to peace and unity." – Nicholas Robertson

Reconciliation embodies the act of aligning, making amends, or harmonising. It requires various parties to converge on a common ground, always accompanied by change. The reconciliation of adversaries necessitates some form of transformation; otherwise, fostering friendship remains implausible.

Christian reconciliation denotes the restoration of a right relationship with God. Before delving further, it's crucial to clarify that our rift with God wasn't caused by any fault on His part. It was our choice to distance ourselves from God, not the reverse (Genesis 3:8). God is flawless while we are flawed (Romans 3:23). He doesn't require alteration, compromise, or seek a midway agreement with us. It's us who need transformation.

Our sin had estranged us, rendering us enemies of God (Romans 5:10). Remarkably, Christ initiated the process to reconcile us to Himself. "In Christ God was reconciling the world to Himself, not counting their trespasses against them, and entrusting to us the message of reconciliation" (2 Corinthians 5:19). God desired our reconciliation knowing we couldn't resolve our sin issue independently. Thus, He provided a way for us to be set right with Him through Christ.

Believers have their sins forgiven, an essential step in reconciling with God. Colossians 1:21-22 attests, "You, who once were alienated and hostile in mind, doing evil deeds, He has now reconciled in His body of flesh by His death, in order to present you holy and blameless and above reproach before Him." We are no longer estranged; instead, forgiven, transformed, and reconciled. Through Jesus' sacrifice, we can commune with God.

Now, instead of viewing us as adversaries, Christ regards us as "friends" (John 15:15). Jesus is our peace; He serves as the mediator ensuring our right standing with God. "Since we have been justified by faith, we have peace with God through our Lord Jesus Christ" (Romans 5:1).

Christ's sacrifice not only provides us peace with God but also fosters peace among fellow believers. Diverse backgrounds, innate conflicts, historical grievances—none of it matters to those reborn in Christ. "There is neither Jew nor Greek, there is neither slave nor free, there is no male and female, for you are all one in Christ Jesus" (Galatians 3:28). Ephesians 2:14-16 underscores God's reconciliation between Jews and Gentiles: "For He Himself is our peace . . . that He might create in Himself one new man in place of the two, so making peace, and might reconcile us both to God in one body through the cross, thereby killing the hostility."

Dear reader,
"Blessed are the peacemakers," affirmed Jesus, knowing it firsthand (Matthew 5:9). He provided a way to exchange our fractured, sinful lives for connected forgiven lives. He transformed enmity into intimacy. As Hosea pursued his unfaithful wife to restore their relationship (Hosea 3), God has pursued us, seeking reconciliation. "He brought me to the banqueting house, and His banner over me was love" (Song of Solomon 2:4).

CLEANSING THE SOUL:
Understanding the Purpose of Confession

"Confession is not just admitting our wrongs; it's humbly acknowledging our need for forgiveness, inviting God's mercy to cleanse and renew our hearts."- Nicholas Robertson

Confession of sin signifies more than a mere acknowledgment of our wrongdoings; it embodies a sincere agreement with God that our actions or words have transgressed His divine law. Drawing a parallel to a courtroom setting, confessing a crime concedes a violation of societal norms. Similarly, when we confess our sins, we acknowledge the breach of God's law, recognising our divergence from His will and acknowledging our culpability before Him.

Linked intimately with confession is repentance. While confession entails admitting the wrongdoing, repentance contains a profound desire for transformative change. It surpasses the mere acknowledgment of sin, urging us to take definitive steps to overcome and forsake it. Confession bereft of genuine repentance becomes hollow; it becomes a mere string of words. Often, individuals may admit their faults when caught red-handed, yet without an authentic intention to amend their ways. Their remorse stems more from facing consequences rather than acknowledging the sin's gravity. John the Baptist's exhortation to "Bear fruit in keeping with repentance" (Matthew 3:8) emphasises not just verbal confession but an evident transformation born out of genuine repentance.

The Bible presents two avenues for the confession of sins. Firstly, it exhorts us to confess our sins to God. First John 1:9 assures that God, being faithful and just, forgives our sins upon our confession and cleanses us from all unrighteousness. Secondly, it advocates confessing our sins to fellow believers. James 5:16 encourages mutual confession among believers for healing and restoration. Moreover, when we wrong someone, confessing to them and seeking forgiveness is the appropriate course of action.

Several impediments can hinder our confession of sins. Pride stands as a significant barrier, often preventing us from admitting our wrongs. It compels us to justify or shift blame, hindering genuine confession and forgiveness. Moreover, ignorance, fuelled by biblical illiteracy, steers individuals away from acknowledging their transgressions against God's standards. Some prefer ignorance to avoid the discomfort of confession and repentance, neglecting God's moral standards at their peril. Ignorance, however, cannot absolve us of the responsibility to confess and seek forgiveness.

Confessing our sins to those we've wronged should always accompany a plea for forgiveness, although forgiveness cannot be coerced. Biblical teachings advocate forgiveness among believers, fostering reconciliation and restoration. Jesus exemplified this through His teachings on confession and restoration within the church (Matthew 18:15–17). Additionally, confession to fellow believers can serve as a means of accountability and change (James 5:16).

Dear reader,
The adage "Confession is good for the soul" rings true, reflecting God's desire for us to live with clear consciences and pure hearts. This necessitates regular confession and forsaking of our sins, emulating Jesus as our model. Though sinless, Jesus's example underscores the importance of confession, reminding us to regularly confess our sins to God and others, thereby liberating ourselves from guilt and shame.

METAMORPHOSIS OF THE SOUL:
Exploring the Transformative Power of Conversion

"Conversion is not just a change of mind; it's a change of heart, a radical transformation that redirects our lives towards God's purposes and His kingdom."- Nicholas Robertson

Conversion, at its core, signifies a profound change, a transformation from one state to another, akin to converting measurements or energy. However, in the spiritual realm, conversion carries a deeper connotation—a reorientation of the heart, mind, and soul.

In the Old Testament, the Hebrew term translated as "converted" implies a return to one's original state, akin to the restoration of one's soul as depicted in Psalm 23:3. It encapsulates the biblical concept of reverting to the intended state of creation.

Since the Fall, humanity has grappled with a sin nature, tending towards self-gratification rather than God's will. Despite our efforts to attain goodness, our imperfections fall short of God's perfection (Romans 3:10, 23; Isaiah 53:6). Faced with this disparity, our own striving cannot bridge the gap, leading to eternal separation from God (Romans 6:23, 8:8; John 3:16-18). This inability to convert ourselves underscores the necessity of Jesus' sacrificial mission—to offer His life for ours, paving the way for redemption and righteousness (1 Corinthians 15:3-4; 2 Corinthians 5:21).

True conversion materialises when, in acknowledging our helplessness, we embrace Christ as our Saviour and Lord (Acts 3:19; Romans 10:9). It involves relinquishing our old sinful nature for the new, provided by Christ. This shift comprises a genuine change in perspective, marked by humility, confession, repentance, and a pursuit of God's ways. The Holy Spirit catalyses this transformation, infusing our lives with a radical newness (Acts 2:38; 1 Corinthians 6:19-20).

Conversion, as articulated in 2 Corinthians 5:17, goes beyond mere self-improvement; it's a complete reversal, a redirection of one's moral compass from sinfulness to righteousness, from a path leading to perdition to one bound for heaven.

The Bible narrates compelling stories of individuals transformed by God's grace—Saul metamorphosed into Paul, the persecutor became the preacher; John, once impulsive and harsh, became the apostle of love. Such conversions continue today—stories abound of lives radically altered by encounters with God's grace.

Faith is the foundation of conversion—trusting in the unseen, acknowledging God's existence, and believing in His promises (Hebrews 11:1, 6). Yet even faith itself is a gift bestowed by God, requiring our reception and activation (Ephesians 2:8-9).

Authentic conversion doesn't stop at words—it permeates one's being, influencing thoughts, speech, and actions. It's a shift from self-centredness to God-centredness, manifesting in an altered life trajectory and allegiance. As the heart undergoes this metamorphosis, actions follow suit, culminating in a life honouring God (James 2:26; Romans 6:6-7).

Finally, conversion encapsulates an intense inward and outward transformation—a complete shift from darkness to light, from self-adoration to worshipping God, marking a life forever altered by divine grace.

Dear reader,
Are you transformed?

SHARING THE LIGHT:
Understanding the Art of Effective Witnessing

"Effective witnessing is not just about speaking; it's about living out our faith in such a way that others are drawn to the light of Christ shining through us."- Nicholas Robertson

In the pursuit of becoming a compelling witness for Christ, understanding the essence of witnessing and its fundamental principles stands paramount. A "witness" substantiates facts through firsthand knowledge. In our context, effective witnessing requires a personal encounter with Christ. John the Apostle, in 1 John 1:1-3, underscores the importance of personal experience, having seen, touched, and experienced the transformative power of Christ. Today, as recipients of His love and forgiveness, our testimony manifests both verbally and through the very fabric of our lives.

To be effective in our witness, certain foundational aspects merit attention:

- **The Theme:**

The foundation of our witness is Jesus Christ Himself. Paul delineated the gospel as centring around the death, burial, and resurrection of Jesus Christ (1 Corinthians 15:1-4). Our proclamation should revolve around the sacrificial act of Christ; failing to convey this crucial aspect dilutes the essence of the gospel (1 Corinthians 2:2; Romans 10:9-10). A pivotal aspect of this theme is the exclusivity of Christ as the singular path to salvation: "I am the way, the truth, and the life. No one comes to the Father except through me" (John 14:6).

- **The Power:**

The Holy Spirit constitutes the dynamic force behind our witness. It is the Spirit who engenders transformation in lives (Titus 3:5), and this transformation becomes evident in our testimonies. Therefore, prayer becomes our stronghold as we seek the Spirit's empowerment, enabling us to radiate God's power in a manner that illuminates His presence within us (Matthew 5:16).

- **The Validity:**

The authenticity of our witness transpires through the way we conduct our lives. Philippians 2:15 sets forth the aspiration for believers to live blamelessly and purely during a morally depraved world, shining as beacons of light. An effective Christian witness lives above reproach, empowered by the Spirit, displaying the fruit that stems from abiding in Christ (John 15:1-8; Galatians 5:22-23).

- **The Scripture and Prayer:**

Crucially, familiarity with Scripture becomes imperative for coherent and accurate presentation of the gospel. As noted in 1 Peter 3:15, readiness to explain the hope within us demands diligent study, Scripture memorisation, and prayer for opportune moments to share the message of salvation with receptive hearts, orchestrated by the Lord.

- **Transformed and Exemplary Living:**

Effective witnessing transcends mere words; it embodies a life transformed by Christ, radiating His love, and standing firm on the foundational truths of the gospel. This witnessing, rooted in personal experience and underpinned by Scripture, becomes a compelling testament to the life-changing power of Christ.

Dear reader,

For more witnessing and evangelism, consider acquiring our book: **Critical Keys for Marketplace Evangelism**

LIBERATED BY GRACE:
Understanding Divine Deliverance

"Divine deliverance is not just an escape from trouble; it's a manifestation of God's power, grace, and faithfulness, leading us from bondage to freedom, from darkness to light."- Nicholas Robertson

Deliverance embodies a rescue from bondage or imminent danger. Throughout the Bible, divine deliverance manifests as God's intervention to rescue His people from perilous situations. In the Old Testament, the focus lies on God's acts of deliverance—be it from enemies, calamities, or impending death. The exodus from Egypt stands as an iconic testament to God's role as the Deliverer of Israel, a manifestation of His boundless mercy and love.

Transitioning to the New Testament, God remains the focal point of deliverance, and His people become its recipients. While the temporal deliverance in the Old Testament symbolises spiritual deliverance from sin through Christ, the New Testament illuminates Christ's pivotal role in delivering humanity from its greatest peril—sin, evil, and eternal judgment. Through Christ, believers experience deliverance from the present evil age and the dominion of Satan, underscoring the exclusive avenue to deliverance (Galatians 1:4; Colossians 1:13). Christ, by His sacrificial act, becomes the epitome of deliverance, rescuing believers from eternal punishment. This eternal deliverance is encapsulated in Romans 4:25, emphasising Christ's deliverance to save humanity from the impending "wrath to come" (1 Thessalonians 1:10). Another facet of deliverance pertains to temporal trials. While believers are permanently delivered from eternal punishment, they encounter temporal trials in life. Sometimes, deliverance involves God walking alongside believers through trials, using these moments to nurture and strengthen faith. This resilience is evident in Paul's assurance to the Corinthians, highlighting God's faithfulness in providing a way out of temptations (1 Corinthians 10:13). This deliverance, however, might not be immediate but unfolds in due time, nurturing patience, and perseverance (James 1:2-4, 12).

Deliverance also extends to spiritual battles against evil influences. While believers possess eternal victory over spiritual adversaries, they seek deliverance from the sway of evil spirits or sinful influences. Equipped with spiritual armour, believers wield the shield of faith and the sword of the Spirit—the Word of God—to thwart spiritual attacks (Ephesians 6:12-17). By wielding faith as a shield, believers deflect spiritual onslaughts, while the Word of God becomes the offensive weapon to counter lies propagated by the enemy (John 8:44; 1 John 2:14).

Dear reader,

Ultimately, deliverance from sin, triumph over trials, and freedom from the clutches of a world under the evil one's influence are found solely in Christ—the embodiment of truth and eternal life (1 John 5:19-20). Divine deliverance encompasses multifaceted facets, all converging upon the redemptive power of Christ, the true source of deliverance in every sphere of life.

ENGAGING IN SPIRITUAL BATTLE:
Examining the Practice of Casting Out Demons

"Casting out demons from others requires discernment, humility, and reliance on God's power, as we engage in spiritual warfare with the authority and guidance of the Holy Spirit." – Nicholas Robertson

Exorcism, derived from the Ancient Greek ἐξορκισμός (exorkismós) meaning 'binding by oath,' constitutes the act of religious or spiritual expulsion of demons, jinns, or malevolent entities believed to possess a person or a place. In biblical narratives, exorcism was practiced by various individuals, including Christ's disciples following His instructions (Matthew 10), others invoking Christ's name (Mark 9:38), the Pharisees' children (Luke 11:18-19), Paul (Acts 16), and specific exorcists (Acts 19:11-16). The disciples' exorcisms aimed to showcase Christ's authority over demons (Luke 10:17) and validate their actions in His name and by His authorisation. These acts also revealed the disciples' level of faith or lack thereof (Matthew 17:14-21). While it was a significant aspect of the disciples' ministry, its precise role in the discipleship process remains unclear.

Interestingly, a shift regarding demonic warfare appears in the latter part of the New Testament. The doctrinal sections (Romans through Jude) acknowledge demonic activity but omit discussions on casting them out, nor do they encourage believers to engage in such actions. Instead, believers are instructed to equip themselves with spiritual armour to resist and stand against demonic forces (Ephesians 6:10-18). They are advised to resist the devil (James 4:7), be vigilant (1 Peter 5:8), and not allow space for him in their lives (Ephesians 4:27). However, explicit directives on casting out demons from others are absent. The book of Ephesians provides clear guidance on achieving victory against evil forces. The initial step involves placing faith in Christ (Ephesians 2:8-9), breaking the dominion of "the prince of the power of the air" (Ephesians 2:2). Subsequently, believers are urged, through God's grace, to shed ungodly behaviours and adopt godly ones (Ephesians 4:17-24). This process focuses on renewing the mind (Ephesians 4:23) rather than casting out demons. Following practical instructions for godly living, believers are reminded of the spiritual battle, fought using spiritual armour to resist, not expel, the cunning of the demonic realm (Ephesians 6:10-18). This armour comprises truth, righteousness, the gospel, faith, salvation, the Word of God, and prayer.

As the completion of the Word of God approached, believers had more effective spiritual weaponry compared to early Christians. Casting out demons was largely replaced by evangelism and discipleship through the Word of God. Given that New Testament spiritual warfare methods do not involve explicit exorcisms, instructions on performing such acts are challenging to discern. If necessary, it seems to involve exposing individuals to the truth of the Word of God and invoking the name of Jesus Christ. Casting out demons was only one of the tools in the believer's toolbox. Whether you use it today or not must be based on the Holy Spirit's guidance.

Dear reader,

The goal of exorcism is to free the afflicted person from spiritual bondage and restore them to health and wholeness; not to garner personal fame.

POSTFACE

As we conclude our journey through **"Nurturing Your Faith: A Guide to Discipleship and Spiritual Growth,"** I want to express my heartfelt gratitude for joining me on this exploration of faith and discipleship. Throughout this guide, we have delved into various aspects of the Christian walk, from understanding the fundamentals of faith to embracing the transformative power of discipleship. It has been a privilege to accompany you as we navigated the pathways of prayer, scripture, community, and service, seeking to deepen our relationship with God and grow in our faith.

In closing, I want to encourage you to continue nurturing your faith journey beyond the pages of this guide. Remember that spiritual growth is not a destination but a lifelong pursuit—a journey marked by moments of joy, challenge, and growth. As you walk in faith, may you remain rooted in God's Word, steadfast in prayer, and committed to serving others with love and compassion. May you seek out opportunities for fellowship and discipleship, surrounding yourself with fellow believers who can support and encourage you along the way.

Above all, may you never lose sight of the incredible privilege we have as followers of Christ—to know Him, to love Him, and to be transformed by His grace. May your faith continue to deepen and mature, bearing fruit in every area of your life and bringing glory to God.

Thank you once again for allowing me to be a part of your journey. May God bless you abundantly as you continue to walk in faith and grow in grace.

With gratitude and blessings,
 Nicholas Robertson
Your Faith Walker

ABOUT THE AUTHOR
Nicholas A Robertson (Director)

NICHOLAS A. ROBERTSON, Dip. Min (Hon.), Dip.Ed. (Hon.), BD (Hon.) B. Ed (Hon.) M.Ed. (Hon.) is a dynamic speaker, counsellor, mentor, and educator who meticulously uses his expertise from military service and his pedagogy to expound on the principles of the Kingdom of God. From as early as 2006, he has been actively involved in ministry and his service transcends borders. To date, he has served in Jamaica, the United States of America, and the United Kingdom. Rev Robertson has operated in the following areas: Youth Ministry, Evangelism, Christian Education, Leadership, Radio, and Social Media ministry.

He studied at the Church Teacher's College, University of the West Indies, Mona, United Theological College of the West Indies, and the Christian Leaders College.

He is the founder of Positive Vibration 365 Plus Global, a daily devotional on social media; co-host of Mr. & Mrs. Robdon's Couples Corner and is also the founder and COO of BuildAMan Foundation Global., a non-profit initiative to develop Godly men, husbands, and fathers. He is also co-founder and director of Impact Online Bible Institute Ltd. He is also the author of Positive Vibration: Navigating through Difficult Times, a book towards equipping persons with the appropriate attitude to navigate life's journey. He is also the author of Positive Vibration: Biblical Keys for Faith Activation. Additionally, he co-authors Critical Keys for Biblical Interpretation: The Believer's Handbook (Book 1 and Book 2)

Nicholas 'Robdon' Robertson is married to Danielle Robertson and they both share two beautiful children: Danick and Danice.

BECOME A STUDENT AT IOBI

We are a subsidiary organisation of the Positive Vibration Global group of ministries dedicated to providing training to the community equipping them to serve areas of ministry within the marketplace.

We offer flexible and affordable tailored to you or your church's demand. These include six weeks courses, webinars, accelerated program, training and support programs, life coaching, leadership, and empowerment programs.

Our courses are thoroughly researched and prepared with you in mind.

Follow the link to register: https://bit.ly/IOBIRegistration

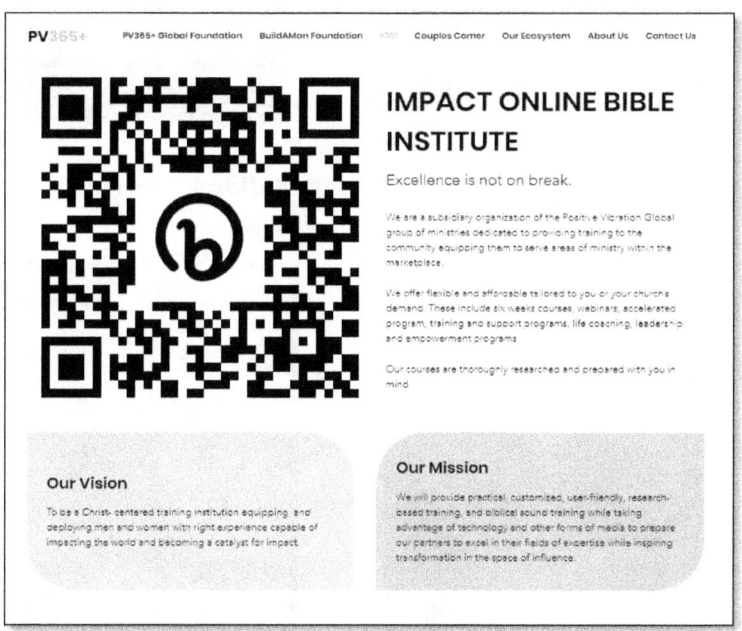

ADDITIONAL RESOURCE

Check out our books from varying categories:

Faith, discipline and growth:

Enduring difficult times

Building Thriving Marriage s:

Building Thriving Marriages:

Leadership, Administration and Management:

Creating Financial Freedom.

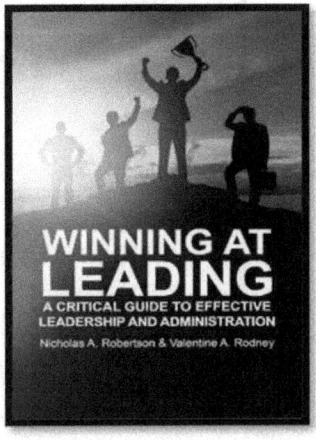

Discipleship, Evangelism, Missions:

Youth empowerment and mentorship

Purpose, Vision, Leadership, Men Empowerment:

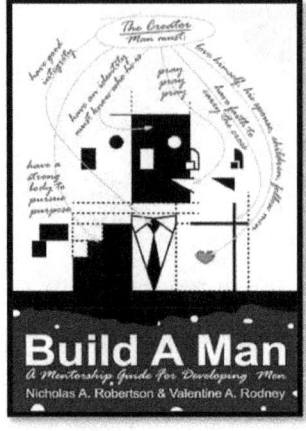

Creating Intimacy in marriage.

Tools for interpreting the Bible:

Tools for interpreting the Bible:

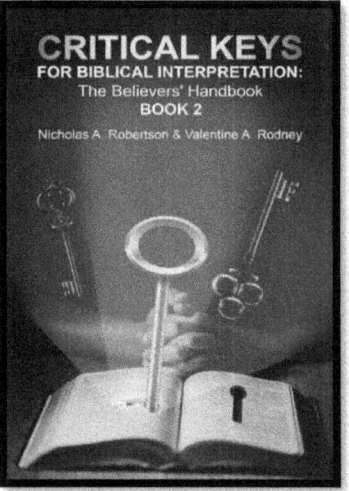

Prayer, reflection, and meditation:

Prayer, reflection, and meditation:

Prayer, reflection, and meditation:

Prayer, reflection, and meditation:

NOTES

- ✓ **Visit our website to order Sign Copies: https://www.positivevibrationglobal.com/shop**
- ✓ Also available on Amazon and Barnes & Noble
- ✓ Contact us on Facebook @Impact Online Bible Institute
- ✓ Email: nrobertson@positivevibrationglobal.com /reasonwithrobdon@gmail.com

www.ingramcontent.com/pod-product-compliance
Lightning Source LLC
Chambersburg PA
CBHW060108170426
43198CB00010B/814